4

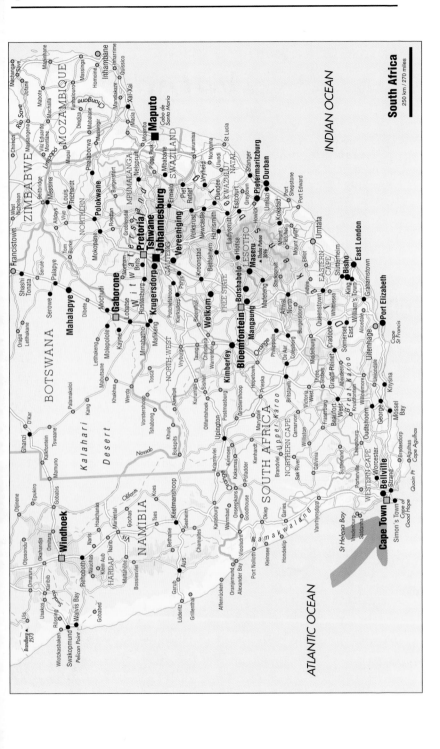

Welcome

This guidebook combines the interests and enthusiasms of two of the world's best-known information providers: Insight Guides, who have set the standard for visual travel guides since 1970, and Discovery Channel, the world's premier source of non-fiction television programming. Its aim is to bring you the best of Cape Town in a series of tailor-made itineraries, put together by native Cape Tonian Paul Duncan.

The guide begins with three full-day itineraries linking the essential sights of the city, beginning with a walking tour of the city centre, then visiting the highlights of the Cape Peninsula, and, on the third day, focusing on the Victoria & Alfred Waterfront. These are followed by five further itineraries designed for visitors with more time to spend in the city, and then five excursions exploring the Cape of Good Hope Nature Reserve, Robben Island, Stellenbosch, the Franschhoek Wine Route, and Darling and the West Coast National Park. The itineraries are supported by sections on history and culture, shopping, eating out and nightlife, a calendar of special events and a fact-packed practical information section which includes a list of hotels.

Paul Duncan has spent much of his life in London and Paris, but he eventually returned to his native South Africa in search of a quieter life – only to find Cape Town humming with activity. The Mother City had shaken off the shackles imposed by the apartheid years and had joined the ranks of those other places defined by their shops, festivals, restaurants, social life, beaches and sunshine-on-the-body-beautiful quotient. Paul Duncan is an editor-in-chief at Conde Nast, whose offices face the foothills of Table Mountain. And when it all gets too much for him, he heads for the hills or the desert, and a remote farm which, just two hours away, could be on another planet.

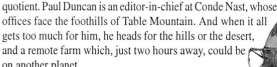

HISTORY AND CULTURE

CITY ITINERARIES

contents

EXCURSIONS

Five short excursions to destinations located beyond the city limits but within easy reach by car.

LEISURE ACTIVITIES

CALENDAR OF EVENTS

PRACTICAL INFORMATION

MAPS

INDEX AND CREDITS

Preceding Pages: the Twelve Apostles rise over Clifton
Following Pages: making a song and dance on Long Street

History *&Culture*

The statue of Jan van Riebeeck must have been a fine sight when, in 1899, it was unveiled at the head of Cape Town's old main pier. Today, dwarfed by the modern megaliths of the city he founded, and covered by its grime, van Riebeeck surveys the handiwork of more than 300 years of human endeavour. Once a primitive hamlet and mud-walled fort, South Africa's mother city has become a melting pot of diverse cultures.

When the Dutch settlers arrived at the Cape in 1652 their first contact was with Khoikhoi farmers. Skulls and stone implements show that the Khoikhoi were preceded by earlier cultures similar to that of the Stone-Age peoples of Europe and India. As the Dutch settlement spread, the colonialists encountered the San, or Bushmen, hunter-gatherers who had lived in the area for thousands of years. There is still considerable debate as to whether there was a break between the earlier cultures and that of the San, or whether, as seems more likely, the San amalgamated with the earlier tribes, as the Khoikhoi subsequently did with the San.

Europe Discovers the Cape

Europeans inadvertently discovered the Cape of Good Hope as a result of Portuguese voyages in search of a sea route to India. In 1487 Bartholomeu Dias sailed round the Cape, which he called the Cape of Storms due to its treacherous coast and fierce weather. His king, Joao II, renamed it the Cape of Good Hope. Ten years after Dias's historic journey, Vasco da Gama became the first explorer to land on Indian soil via the Cape; the Portuguese fleets had found the route to riches.

In 1503, Portugal's Antonio de Saldanha became the first European to climb the Cape's Table Mountain. Initially the Portuguese made no effort to establish a settlement in the area. Not only was the stormy Cape notorious among mariners, but a series of violent clashes with the Khoikhoi seemed to reinforce European doubts about trade links with the indigenous people.

By 1590 the Dutch controlled the trade route to India, largely through the Dutch East India Company (Vereenigde Oost-Indische Compagnie or VOC), which was established to control mercantile business in the new colonies. In 1647 the Dutch ship *Haerlem* ran aground in Table Bay, leaving some of the crew stranded for a year before being rescued. As a result of the shipwreck, VOC directors began to realise the value of a permanent settlement in the Cape. The Dutch, however, had no intention of colonising the coun-

Left: San rock art. **Right:** San hunters, from a painting by Samuell Daniell, about 1830.

try, but were content to establish a refreshment station there.

In 1652 the VOC sent a small expedition, led by van Riebeeck, to secure a source of fresh water and to plant vegetable gardens in the Cape. The expeditionaries built a fort on the site of modern Cape Town's Grand Parade and planted gardens that formed the basis of today's Botanical or Company's Gardens. The Castle of Good Hope, built between 1666 and 1679, replaced van Riebeeck's fort and is today the oldest European structure in southern Africa. Persevering against all odds, van Riebeeck's little settlement began to take shape. The community's mostly Dutch VOC employees belonged to either the tiny elite force of officers or, overwhelmingly, the main body of ill-educated soldiers and sailors, many of whom had been pressed into service.

Birth of the Trekboer

In 1657 the settlement commander persuaded the VOC directors to discharge a few servants, letting them become 'free burghers' entitled to farm specially allocated land. The intention was to produce crops for the company. The VOC wanted to command the cattle trade with the Khoikhoi, to maximise its own profits and to prevent clashes between Khoikhoi and settlers. But the settlers could not be prevented from raising their own cattle, and the migratory frontiersman, the Trekboer, came into existence. Essentially itinerant herdsmen, the Trekboer never stayed in one place long enough to plant crops. Meanwhile a settled agricultural society based on wheat crops and wineries had developed to the west. The wine industry was created by French Huguenot refugees, who arrived in 1688 and who intermarried with the Dutch settlers.

Van Riebeeck solved the labour shortage by importing slaves from India, Madagascar, Ceylon, Malaya and Indonesia. The Muslim influence is evident

history/culture

today in the suburbs' many mosques; and the city lies within a mystical circle of Muslim shrines reputed to protect it from natural disasters. By the end of the 18th century, South African society – whites, Khoikhoi and slaves – was forming the basis of today's Cape Coloured population. The San had been practically wiped out by conflicts with the Khoikhoi and descendants of the European settlers (known as Afrikaners or Boers). The Khoikhoi, decimated by smallpox epidemics in 1713 and 1755, were dispersed.

British Colonisation

In 1795, during the French Revolutionary wars, Britain seized the Cape to prevent its use by France, which was then allied to Holland. The colony was returned to the Dutch in 1803 but was again occupied by the British in 1806. The 1814–15 Congress of Vienna ceded the colony to the British on a permanent basis. Britain introduced a number of reforms including, in 1834, the emancipation of slaves, many of whom settled in the Bo-Kaap on the eastern slopes of Signal Hill. The remaining Khoisan, who were treated as slaves, were finally given the explicit protection of the law (including the right to own land) in 1828. Neither move suited the type of society being developed by whites at the Cape. The result was a series of conflicts that resulted in the colony's mass emigration, the Great Trek of 1834–1840.

Although Britain was responsible for ridding the Cape of slavery, its new labour laws laid the basis for an exploitative system barely more liberal than the system it had abolished. Pass laws prevented thousands of dispossessed blacks from acquiring work in the colony. And the 'multiracial' constituency of a parliament established in the Cape in 1854 excluded the vast majority of non-whites who could not meet the financial criteria of suffrage.

Suburban development, largely inland to the east and down the Cape peninsula to the south, followed the construction of radial roads and the railway line, which began in 1859. The Alfred Dock (where the Victoria & Alfred Waterfront complex is situated today) opened in 1870 and was a boon to shipping. Immigrants were attracted by the discovery, inland, of diamonds in 1870 and gold in 1886. The industrialisation of Cape Town had begun.

Afrikaner hostility to Britain was growing in the Cape Colony, especially after the first British annexation of the Transvaal in 1877. Afrikaners began to organise politically: in 1881 the formation of the Afrikaner Bond expressed the avowed aim of expelling the British from South Africa. This organisation did not remain anti-British for very long – in 1890 it supported Cecil John Rhodes's successful campaign to become prime minister of the Cape Colony. Rhodes, whose wealth derived from his position at the head of De Beers Consolidated Mines, pursued his dream of imperial expansion until the disastrous Jameson Raid of 1895.

Above Left: a typical Boer frontier family with Khoisan servants in attendance
Left: Table Bay in 1683. **Above:** a British infantryman at Batavia in 1803

Rhodes sponsored this rebellion against President Kruger's South African Republic (Transvaal) and its failure forced his resignation.

The raid divided Boer and Briton more than ever (as well as triggering a surge of African nationalism) and the Anglo-Boer War of 1899–1902 was unavoidable. The Cape played a pivotal role in the war as it provided vital aid to the imperial troops. In the wake of the war, Lord Milner, the British High Commissioner of the Cape, tried to rehabilitate the devastated former South African provinces as crown colonies under the framework of an enlarged British South Africa, a policy codified by the Union Act of 1910.

In the following years, the Cape's influence in South Africa diminished. Although Cape Town was made the legislative capital of the new state, the administrative capital was established at Pretoria in the Transvaal. Revenue declined, and the economic growth of the Transvaal outstripped that of the Cape. The white population of the Cape ceased to expand, and the province lost its status as the most populous in the country. The Cape's liberal franchise

laws, which granted the vote to non-whites, was not extended to other provinces as Cape leaders had hoped. Eventually blacks lost the right to vote in 1936; 'coloureds' in 1956. In 1912 the South African Native Congress (renamed the African National Congress, ANC, in 1923) was formed to create African unity and to fight for political rights. Until the 1950s, its strategy was one of passive resistance; its appeals to government were less proactive than reactive.

The Rise of Apartheid

It was a divided South Africa that joined the Allies embarking on World War II in September 1939. While those figures who opposed the war effort were making their voice heard, prime minister Jan Smuts was busy uniting the conflict's supporters in a coalition government. Unfortunately for his own political career, Smuts underestimated the considerable amount of grass-roots backing D F Malan's National Party had among the predominantly Afrikaner white population. The National Party's apartheid ('apartness' in Afrikaans) policies of rigorous segregation between whites and blacks was popular with increasing numbers of a white population which feared that its jobs were threatened by the cheap black labour force.

The post-war 1948 election resulted in a National Party-Afrikaner Party coalition. The new government immediately set about legislating for colour segregation, which had been a de facto part of South Africa's culture for generations. Laws classified the country's people into colour categories, with severe restrictions on the lives, livelihoods and movements of non-whites, a sector of the population now obliged to carry passes. The government introduced a system of independent homelands, to which all black South Africans were forced to belong. Only blacks in possession of work passes

Above: prime minister Hendrik Verwoerd, who was assassinated in parliament in 1966

were allowed to reside inside 'white South Africa', and even members of this privileged minority were classified as citizens of one of the homelands.

The Cape Coloureds were not granted a homeland – the western half of the Cape province was declared a 'coloured preference area' in which no black could be employed unless it could be proved that there was no suitable coloured person for the job. Whenever the illegal black squatter camps mushroomed on the sandy plains to the east of Cape Town, they would be flattened by government bulldozers, their occupants dragged away and dumped in their homelands. Within weeks the shanties would rise again.

In 1960 the ANC, together with its radical offshoot, the Pan Africanist Congress (PAC), organised marches against the hated pass laws. At Langa and Nyanga near Cape Town, police killed five protesters, and a warrant to arrest Nelson Mandela and other ANC leaders was issued. In 1963 Mandela was captured, tried and sentenced to life imprisonment. Like many black leaders before him, he was incarcerated on Robben Island in Table Bay.

District Six

Visible reminders of apartheid can sometimes be seen in places such as public toilets, where the words 'European' or 'Non-European' are etched, though most such signs have been removed by collectors. But District Six, to the east of the city centre, remains a symbol of one of the most traumatic periods of the apartheid era. This had been a particularly vibrant, ethnically and religiously cosmopolitan community that suffered none of the social alienation that troubled other, comparably diverse parts of the country. Jazz music was its lifeblood, and the district was home to many musicians, including the legendary Dollar Brand (aka Abdullah Ibrahim). The proximity to Cape Town allowed the city itself to benefit from its vitality.

In 1966, under the aegis of the Group Areas Act, the government declared District Six a 'white' area, and began the forcible removal of a community of 60,000 people to townships on the Cape Flats. For all the community's active resistance, the government was implacable: over the following decade

Above: rioting and public violence were a hallmark of the apartheid years

eviction notices were served and the bulldozers demolished homes and shops. By 1982 all that remained were a few places of worship and a pile of bricks. In 1994 former residents of the area established the District Six Museum to reclaim the history of this area and its people.

The government also tried to eradicate squatter towns, such as Crossroads, which were focal points for black resistance to apartheid. In May–June 1986, an estimated 70,000 people were driven from their homes and hundreds were killed. This brutal series of attacks was unsuccessful and, in the face of an international outcry, the government performed a volte-face and reluctantly began to upgrade living conditions for blacks. As a result, vast new townships have grown at Khayelitsha and Mitchell's Plain.

Mandela's Release

By 1987 economic decline, coupled with a rise in black opposition to white rule, made the obvious need for change all the more urgent: the transformation of the country's political landscape in the 1990s was surely inevitable. In February 1990, President de Klerk revoked the bans on black political parties, and over the next year, he introduced a number of similar reforms, culminating in the release of Nelson Mandela, after 27 years' imprisonment.

On 16 April 1994, the first genuinely democratic, nonracial general election in the country's history resulted in a landslide victory for the ANC, and Nelson Mandela was elected president. Hope, although still fragile, began to bloom.

Mandela, with whom the new South Africa has so closely identified, retired from office in 1999 and from public life in 2004. The country recently celebrated 10 years of freedom and has been selected to host the 2010 FIFA World Cup. For all the scars of the past and the long, often painful process of transition, today's South Africa enjoys unprecedented political and social freedom. Cape Town's Houses of Parliament are home to a government that represents all of the country's peoples and plays a key role in global affairs.

HISTORY HIGHLIGHTS

30000BC San hunter-gatherers, probably descendants of a later Stone-Age people, live in South Africa area.

AD300 Emergence of Khoikhoi tribespeople, closely related to the San.

900 Iron-Age Bantu-speaking tribes, probably ancestors of the Xhosa, settled in the coastal grasslands in the far east of the Western Cape region.

1487 Portuguese explorer Bartholomeu Dias rounds the Cape, which is named the Cape of Good Hope.

1498 Vasco da Gama completes the route to India via the Cape.

1503 Antonio de Saldanha anchors at Table Bay and encounters the Khoisan.

1580 Francis Drake reaches the Cape.

1647 The Dutch vessel *Haerlem* is wrecked in Table Bay. Survivors bring back glowing reports of the region.

1652 The Dutch East India Company sends Jan van Riebeeck to the Cape to establish a station.

1657 The station becomes a permanent settlement when company servants are granted their own farms.

1658 The first major group of slaves arrive from the Dutch East Indies.

1679 Simon van der Stel is appointed commander of the Cape settlement.

1688 Arrival of 200 French Huguenots.

1713 First smallpox epidemic hits the Khoisan community.

1755 Second smallpox epidemic all but wipes out the Khoisan.

1795–1803 British occupy Cape Town.

1814–15 Cape Colony ceded to the British by the Congress of Vienna.

1834 Cape slaves are emancipated.

1834–1840 The Great Trek.

1854 The Cape establishes its own representative parliament.

1870 Diamonds are discovered in Griqualand West; Alfred Dock opens.

1886 Gold discovered in the Transvaal.

1890 Cecil John Rhodes becomes prime minister of the Cape Colony.

1895 Jameson Raid; Rhodes resigns.

1899–1902 The Anglo-Boer War.

1910 Crown colonies unite as Union of South Africa with the Cape as the legislative capital.

1936 Black voters in the Cape are disenfranchised.

1939 World War II breaks out. South Africa joins the Allies.

1948 New National Party government launches policy of colour segregation.

1956 Cape Coloureds lose voting rights.

1960 ANC and PAC march against pass laws. Protestors killed at Langa and Nyanga. Warrants issued for arrest of ANC leaders.

1961 The Cape becomes a province of the Republic of South Africa.

1963 ANC leader Nelson Mandela is sentenced to life imprisonment.

1966 60,000 residents of District Six are forcibly removed. Prime minister Verwoerd assassinated in parliament.

1983 New constitution gives coloureds and Asians limited rights.

1989 F W de Klerk becomes president.

1990 Mandela is released.

1991 Apartheid is officially dissolved.

1993 Mandela and F W de Klerk receive Nobel Peace Price.

1994 The first democratic general election results in a landslide victory for the ANC. Nelson Mandela elected president.

1995 South Africa wins rugby's World Cup – a boon to a traumatised nation.

1998 Truth and Reconciliation Commission hearings.

1999 Mandela retires; Thabo Mbeki becomes president following ANC general election victory.

2003 The bungalow at Victor Verster Prison where Mandela spent the last 18 months of his imprisonment is turned into a museum.

2004 Celebration to mark 10 years of freedom. South Africa selected to host 2010 FIFA World Cup.

history/culture

Above Left: Nelson Mandela, South Africa's first black president
Left: a first-time voter proudly displays proof of her newly-won democratic rights

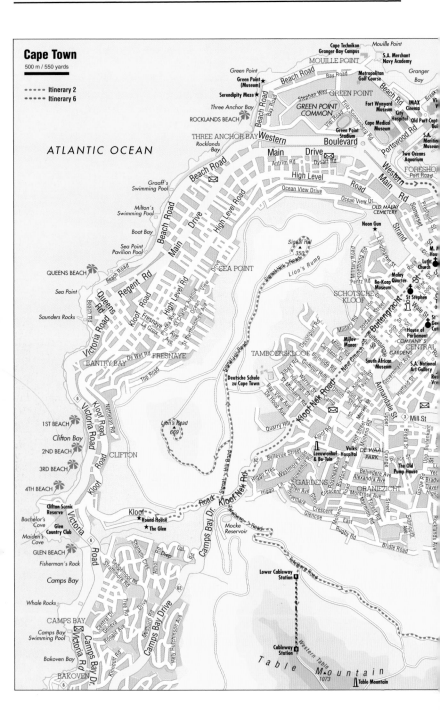

Cape Town

500 m / 550 yards

- – – – – Itinerary 2
- – – – – Itinerary 6

ATLANTIC OCEAN

Mouille Point

Cape Technikon
Granger Bay Campus

S.A. Merchant
Navy Academy

MOUILLE POINT

Green Point
Green Point
(Museum)

Beach Road

Bay Road

Metropolitan
Golf Course

Granger
Bay

Serendipity Maze

Three Anchor Bay

ROCKLANDS BEACH

Beach Road

Bay Road

Stephan Way

GREEN POINT

Fort Wynyard
Museum

INAX
Cinema

Breakw

V;tl Road

Erfl Sonnenberg Rd

GREEN POINT
COMMON

City
Hospital

Old Port Capt
Bui

THREE ANCHOR BAY Western

Green Point
Stadium

Cape Medical
Museum

S.A.
Maritim
Museum

Rocklands
Bay

Main

Drive

Boulevard

Portswood Rd

Two Oceans
Aquarium

Western
Rd

FORESHO
Port Road

Graaff's
Swimming Pool

Beach Road

Antrim Rd

Dysart Rd

High Level

Main

Ocean View Drive

Road

Ocean View Dr.

Fl

Somerset

OLD MALAY
CEMETERY

Strand

Milton's
Swimming Pool

Drive

High Level Road

Noon Gun

Longmarket St

M.
Hou

Luth
Church

Boat Bay

Sea Point
Pavilion Pool

Signal Hill
△ 350

Military Road

Bo-Kaap
Museum

Pentz Rd

Malay
Quarter

QUEENS BEACH

Beach Road

Lion's Rump

Signal Hill Road

SCHOTSCHE
KLOOF

St Stephen

Queens Beach

Regent Rd

SEA POINT

Jordaan Street

House of
Parliament

St Ge

Sl

Saunders Rocks

Queens
Rd

Kloof Road

High Level Rd

Ocean View

St Charles Avenue

Arthurs Ave

Fresnaye Ave

La Croix Ave

Military St

Buitengracht

COMPANY'S
GARDENS

CENTRAL

Fl

Victoria Road

De Wet Rd

FRESNAYE

BANTRY BAY

Top Road

Bartholomew Ave

Signal Hill Road

Kloof Nek Road

TAMBOERSKLOOF

Belmont Ave

Gilmour Hill

Burnside Rd

Milner Rd

New Church

South African
Museum

S.A. National
Art Gallery

Rus

Deutsche Schule
zu Cape Town

Albert Rd

St Michael's Rd

View St

Eaton Rd

Amandale St

Hatfield St

Lion's Head
669

The Hoop Ave

Camp

Kloof Rd

Mill St

Bellevue Street

Prince St

Buitenkant

1ST BEACH

Clifton Bay

Victoria Road

Quarry Hill

Leeuwenhof
& Bo-Tuin

Volks
Hospital

DE WAAL
PARK

The Old
Pump House

2ND BEACH

Kloof Road

Higgos Cres.

Westmore Rd

Leeuwenhof Rd

Rosmead Ave

Belvedere Ave

ORANJEZICHT

Yed

Brad

3RD BEACH

CLIFTON

82

Welgemeend

Alexandra Ave

Daver

4TH BEACH

Higgo

Crescent

Montrose Ave

Clifton Scenic
Reserve

GARDENS

Green Ave

Molteno Rd

Bachelor's
Cove

Glen
Country Club

Kloof

Round House
★

The Glen

Camps Bay Dr.

Kloof Nek Rd

Watermark

Crescent

East

Bridle Road

Maiden's
Cove

Road

Mocke
Reservoir

Glencoe

Rugby Rd

GLEN BEACH

Fisherman's Rock

Signal Hill Road

Road

Kloof

Victoria

Camps Bay

6

Whale Rocks

Shanklin Cres

Athol

Drop

Dal

82

Tafelberg Road

Lower Cableway
Station

CAMPS BAY

Camps Bay
Swimming Pool

Victoria Rd

Camps Bay Drive

Schoonder Road

Geneva

Ronald Ave

Medburn Rd

Central Dr

Kenilworth

Berkley Rd

Hely Hutchinson Ave

Western Table

Bakoven Bay

BAKOVEN

6

Table Mountain

Cableway
Station

Table △ Mountain
1073

△ Table Mountain

City Itineraries

1. THE CITY CENTRE *(see map, p22)*

A leisurely day's walk through the centre of the city taking in historic buildings, markets, the Company's Gardens and the Houses of Parliament. There are lots of places en route to stop for a drink, or lunch.

Start at the top of Government Avenue, cross Annandale Street to the gates of The Mount Nelson Hotel, and finish at the top of St George's Mall, by St George's Cathedral.

A stroll down **Government Avenue**, one of the city centre's most pleasant streets, will take you beneath elderly oaks and past cannas, hydrangeas and agapanthus, with lots of squirrels for company. Shops tend to open at 8.30am, so start early, before it gets too hot. As always in South Africa, watch out for your handbag and camera, don't wear flashy jewellery, and, for all the avenue's seemingly pacific charms, you shouldn't take this walk at night. Government Avenue describes a straight line to the top of Adderley Street, which connects the seaward section of the Company's Gardens to the sea.

The walk leads through the heart of the **Company's Gardens**, which were laid out in 1652 by Jan van Riebeeck and the Dutch East India Company. At the time, 18ha (45 acres) of land were set aside to supply fresh produce for ships sailing from Europe to the Far East. Of this huge market garden, only 3.2ha (8 acres) have survived, of which a chunk was transformed into a public garden by Sir Herbert Baker. Amongst the garden's notable vegetation is a saffron pear tree that, dating from van Riebeeck's day, is said to be the country's oldest cultivated tree. A fenced-off section apart, the park is open to the public from 7am to dusk, daily. There are numerous lovely places where you can sit and relax or walk quietly. There's also a collection of statues and a good view from Government Avenue into the rose gardens that front the garden facade of the Tuynhuis.

Early Maps

The **Houses of Parliament** are at the bottom of Government Avenue in a quiet, almost bucolic scene. The exterior of the parliament edifice (built in 1884) is somewhat nondescript, but the interior houses fine collections of paintings and early maps of the continent, particularly southern Africa. Hour-long tours (weekdays 9am–noon; tel: 021-403 2201) give you the opportunity to view the historic chambers, learn about South African politics – especially the nation's transition from apartheid to democracy – and to ask questions. Ask to see the collection of maps in the Speaker's office.

Left: a covered walkway in Long Street
Right: Company's Gardens war memorial

The President's Office

Next to the Houses of Parliament is the **Tuynhuis**, or president's office. Formerly called Government House, this historic building used to serve as the Cape governor's residence. It was built in the 18th century and converted into an English-style country residence by the governor, Lord Somerset. The overblown architecture you see today was restored in the 1970s.

Just across Government Avenue from the Tuynhuis is the **National Library of South Africa** (Mon–Fri 9am–5pm; tel: 021-424 6320). Founded in 1818, it is one of the world's oldest free libraries. Also serving as the national reference library, it is an important cultural institution that contains many fine collections of books, maps, prints, drawings and manuscripts, such as first editions of works by Shakespeare and Spenser, and an original, 14th-century Dante manuscript. The statue at the front of the building is of the governor Sir George Grey, whose priceless collection of manuscripts and books formed the basis of the library's works when it opened.

Continue to the bottom of Government Avenue, and head on down Adderley Street, passing the Old Slave Lodge, home to the Cultural History Museum. Keep to the right of the street, cross Bureau Street and you'll find yourself in front of the **Groote Kerk**. In 1700, the foundations were laid outside the Castle of Good Hope's walls for the Cape's first permanent church. (Christian services had

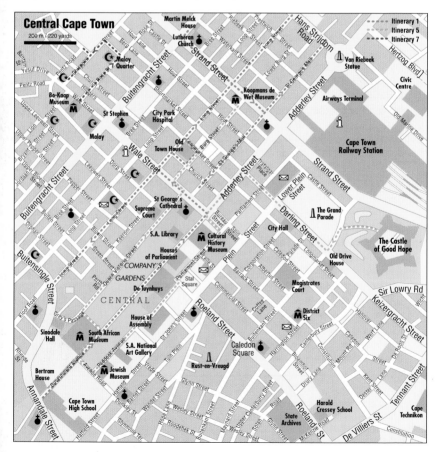

been held in a cabin on van Riebeeck's ship, the *Dromedaris*, and in a room in the castle). Anton Anreith was commissioned to carve the pulpit, which is still in use, and the first stone was laid by Governor van der Stel. Though the bell dates from 1726, only the tower of the original church survived the rebuilding work of 1841. Today the mother church of South Africa's Dutch Reformed community is a half-Grecian, half-Gothic affair surrounded by modern buildings.

Archbishop Tutu

Retrace your steps to the bottom of Government Avenue, turning towards Wale Street with Signal Hill in the distance. To the left you will see the Anglican **St George's Cathedral** (open during daylight hours). In 1901 the architect Sir Herbert Baker began work on the cathedral alongside the original St George's Church. The 19th-century church was deemed superfluous to the needs of the community and demolished in 1954. The destruction of the church was a huge loss to the city, not least because the cathedral that was intended to replace it is hardly Baker's finest achievement. Its Gothic style, complete with long choir and short transept, looks rather odd against the backdrop of a clear blue sky and Table Mountain. Inside, Lord Louis Mountbatten is commemorated in stained glass (the Christ in Majesty in the transept) but, taken as a whole, this still incomplete cathedral

is something of a travesty. The flamboyant Archbishop Desmond Tutu, the cathedral's former resident prelate, operated his anti-government campaign from here, and the funeral of Joe Slovo, the anti-apartheid campaigner, ANC leader and later minister of housing, was held here in December 1994.

Continue up Wale Street and you will arrive at **Long Street**, intersecting it at right angles. Stretching from sea to mountain, Long Street presents a picture of the city's history. You can still see a significant number of two-storey, 19th-century buildings with upper floors that lean out over the pavement, providing passers-by with a covered walkway. The longest sections of these houses are at the mountain end of the street.

Long Street is an exuberant, colourful conglomeration of shops, bars, clubs, restaurants, mosques, churches, street

Above: strolling in Company's Gardens
Right: 19th-century Long Street architecture

vendors, muggers, transvestites, prostitutes and, minding his own business, Joe Public. In the old days, before highways cut off the city from the ocean, the street's most interesting sections were found down near the port. Nowadays, however, it's advisable to stick to the upper sections, where life spills out onto the pavements and there's plenty to see, do and buy. At the very top of Long Street you might want to go for the heat and steam of the **Turkish baths** (women: Mon, Thurs, Sat; men: Tues, Wed, Fri, Sun, 8.30am–8.30pm).

Retrace your steps down Long Street, crossing Wale Street once again and a block later you'll find Church Street. This small road features antiques shops that sell everything from old books and bath tubs to diamond necklaces and feather dusters. The mid-section, between Long Street and Burg Street, is closed to traffic and has a daily bric-a-brac market. The pedestrian area is good for jewellery, glassware and china, the excellent Bukhara restaurant *(see Eating Out, page 69)* and, for al fresco snacks and drinks, Mozart's Café.

At the bottom of the pedestrianised area, head left into Burg Street, which leads into **Greenmarket Square** in the heart of the city. Under the gaze of the historic Old Town House *(see Itinerary 5, page 36)*, the square is the second-oldest in Cape Town. Originally a produce market (founded 1710), it's now a flea market with books, new and second-hand clothes, jewellery, tribal artefacts and junk. There are a number of places to eat and drink around the square.

Above: Greenmarket Square flea market
Left: inside the Old Town House

Exit the square via the seaward section of Burg Street and continue until you reach Strand Street. Head left and continue for four blocks, past the Koopman's de Wet House Museum on the left, until you reach the **Lutheran Church** (Mon–Fri 8.30am–12.30pm; the country's first) – and, next door on the right, **Martin Melck House**. These buildings, which date back to 1778, mark the progress of religious freedom in the colony. German immigrants had been allowed to worship only in the Dutch Reformed Church before Martin Melck, a wealthy merchant of German origin, built a warehouse for them. In 1791 this was transformed into the church you see today.

Look out for the pretty belfry and the finely carved pulpit (finished in 1785) in an interior that is a treasury of 18th- and 19th-century decorative arts. The pulpit is the work of Anton Anreith, as is the building's facade, although this was much altered during the following century. A typical 18th-century town house, Martin Melck House has not been treated kindly by time: in recent years it has been put to use as a nightclub and a kitchen showroom. Today it lies vacant. With the Netherlands Embassy on the church's other side, this trinity of buildings forms the most important group of historical monuments in South Africa.

Running parallel to Adderley Street, Cape Town's main street, St George's Street has been transformed into **St George's Mall**, a pedestrianised area lined with department stores, boutiques, shops, restaurants, cafes and bars, banks and currency exchanges. Street vendors sell a wide range of goods, from sausage rolls to gold jewellery and African baskets. Street musicians, actors and dancers do their own variety of things, so there's plenty to keep you occupied here for hours.

2. AROUND THE MOUNTAINS
(see map, p18–19)

A morning's mountain tour by car, then a walk over boulders. Wear boots or sneakers that grip.

Drive up Buitengracht Street until it becomes New Church Street and the Kloof Nek, which climbs towards the 'neck' between Lion's Head and Table Mountain. Here turn right to drive along Signal Hill, or left, along Tafelberg Road, past the cable-car station and on to the car park at the foot of Devil's Peak.

If you are healthy and fit, you may be able to run up the 670-m (2,200-ft) **Lion's Head** and down the other side in 40 minutes. Plenty of people do just that every day – but be warned: though exhilarating, the climb is almost vertical. The ascent is popular at dawn and dusk; seen from the summit or even the flanks, sunrise and sunset are equally magnificent.

The name, Lion's Head, is something of a mystery. Some say that the Cape peninsula's last lion was shot on its slopes, others that its profile looks like a

Right: you don't have to travel far to find superb beaches

lion's head – which it does (Signal Hill is the rump). Leave your car in the car park at the bottom and follow the path. The views over the Cape Flats to the Hottentots Holland are spectacular, as are those looking down over the Atlantic seaboard. In the early years a watchman stationed at the summit would fire a cannon when a ship approached to alert farmers in outlying areas that provisions for trade should be brought to town.

Gunshot at Noon

The long and relatively low (335m/1,100ft) Signal Hill divides Green Point and Sea Point from the city centre. (To reach the Points and the Atlantic seaboard, either drive up over Kloof Nek or around the seaward-facing point of the hill.) On its slopes is the **Lion's Battery**, which in former times fired salutes to passing ships. The battery also helped ships to correct their chronometers and, after 1918, marked a two-minute silence in honour of South Africa's World War I fallen soldiers. Now a gun is fired every day (except Sunday) at noon. If you get the chance, drive along Signal Hill at dusk, or after dark, to admire the wonderful night-time views.

On the way, check out the **Kramat**, a modest square, white building topped

by a green dome, to which many devout Muslims make pilgrimages. Constructed over the tomb of Goolam Muhamed Soofi, this is one of six similar edifices – the others are on the slopes of Table Mountain, on Robben Island, in Constantia, and in Oudekraal – that form a circle around the Cape peninsula and are reputed to give Cape Town spiritual protection against natural disasters. The parking area at the end of the drive is a good place from which to see Robben Island.

The undoubted highlight of Cape Town's characterful topography is the flat-topped, often cloud-covered **Table Mountain**. The beautiful drive around the mountain, and one or two of the walks, incorporate magnificent views. The cable-car trip is also highly recommended. One of the world's most famous landmarks, the 1,086-m (3,475-ft) mountain can be seen from about 200km (125 miles) out to sea. Its renown attracted sailors to the fledgling settlement beneath its slopes and thus the mountain itself can take credit for the growth of The Tavern of the Seas, as Cape Town came to be known. Composed of hard sandstone, with the main body sitting on a granite pedestal, the mountain is 400–500 million years old.

There are lots of pleasant walks and climbs in and around Table Mountain's ravines. Since what is reputed to be the first European's ascent – by the Portuguese Antonio de Saldanha in 1503 – thousands of hardy souls have braved what are in some instances very dangerous routes. If you want to climb the mountain, you are advised first to take advice from the Mountain Club (tel: 021-465 3412). Most of the walks are well signposted and several are graded according to their degree of difficulty. Avoid stepping out on misty or windy days.

Above: the 'cloth-covered' Table Mountain is one of the world's great landmarks
Above Right: nature-reserve baboons look out to sea. **Right:** the Kramat

For the less adventurous, the cable car (operating Oct–Apr: 8am–8pm, May–Sep: 8.30am–6pm; tel: 021-424 5148), built in 1929 and modernised in the late 1990s, provides a rather more relaxing route to the top. You can park your vehicle in the parking area provided and, once at the summit, enjoy a light lunch or dinner at the restaurant, or tea, coffee and snacks at the café. There are several viewing platforms and clearly defined walking areas.

Baboons, Goats and Dassies

The views from the summit are truly stupendous. To one side, when the weather's clear, you can see all the way to Cape Point. On the other, the west coast slithers off over the horizon in the direction of Namibia. Then there are the Hottentots Holland Mountains that divide the peninsula from the interior. On the way up keep an eye open for baboons, Himalayan mountain goats and mountain dassies; when you're at the top, you might see why the region is famous for the range and variety of its plant species.

About 1,500 of the 2,285 plant species that make up the Cape Floral Kingdom are found on Table Mountain. The early 19th-century English naturalist William Burchill wrote that the rich diversity of plants on these mountain slopes was like 'a botanic garden, neglected and left to grow to a state of nature; so great was the variety everywhere to be met with'.

Today's botanists recognise three kinds of indigenous vegetation on Table Mountain. *Fynbos* (low shrubs and bushes) cover the greatest area, including the upper plateau, patches of forest cling to the south- and east-facing slopes, and you can find remnants of Renosterveld (dominated by daisies) on Signal Hill. Look out for the lovely *Disa uniflora* (a wild orchid) that grows in wet areas, generally around streams and waterfalls. On no account pick this bloom – heavy fines

are intended to dissuade anyone thinking of molesting the mountain's flora. The area's proteas are also celebrated, and there are enough specimens to keep amateur botanists busy for hours. In particular, look out for the delicate ericas (heathers) and the swaying restios (reeds).

The 'Cloth' Phenomenon

When, as frequently happens, the peaks of the mountain are covered by a blanket of clouds, the cable car is closed. Known as the 'cloth' phenomenon, this is caused by the difference in temperature between the air at the summit and that at the bottom of the mountain. The clouds are a manifestation of the 'Cape Doctor' – the notoriously strong southeasterly wind that howls its way around the peninsula between November and March. This notorious wind has been known to sustain speeds of up to 120 kph (75 mph) which, to the uninitiated, can be a shock. In summer, Cape Town is one of the three windiest cities in the world.

As you face Table Mountain, the 1,000-m (3,280-ft) **Devil's Peak** lies to your left. To reach the viewing place at its base, which includes a car-park, continue along the Tafelberg Road, past the cable station. Just underneath you, the King's Blockhouse has the ruins of an 18th-century fort built during the first British occupation of the Cape. These ruins are better preserved than those of the Queen's Blockhouse and the Prince of Wales Blockhouse, both of which are also in the vicinity.

Spread out way beneath the **Twelve Apostles** – a chain of a dozen mountainous peaks (*see the photograph on pages 2–3*) – are the seaside neighbourhoods of Camps Bay – from Kloof Nek, look to the left. When you go over the top, branch right into Kloof Road, just below the way to Signal Hill, and continue down beneath Lion's Head to Clifton, Bantry Bay and then Sea Point. On the way down the mountain, the road passes the 18th-century **Round House**, built on the foundations of one of the batteries that once guarded Cape Town. When the battery fell into disuse, it was turned into a hunting box by the late 18th-century governor Lord Charles Somerset. Even today, the Round House's central room is fitted with four gun cupboards. The building also includes a mediocre restaurant.

Above: Devil's Peak
Right: a modern woman in traditional dress

3. A WALK ON THE WATERFRONT *(see map, p31)*

A leisurely morning walk around the Victoria & Alfred Waterfront with its fine Victorian architecture and interesting shops and restaurants.

Begin at the seaward entrance to the Victoria Wharf Shopping Centre which overlooks the Victoria Basin.

The Victoria Wharf Shopping Centre is full of excellent shops on two levels (daily, 9am–9pm). Here, the port has a direct link with the entertainment area; indeed the Waterfront is a somewhat unusual combination of working port and entertainment centre. Cape Town's original harbour was named after Queen Victoria and her son Prince Alfred, who visited the Cape in 1860, and, following the examples of Boston and San Francisco, its restoration retained the harbour's Victorian character. Hop on a boat in this area for a voyage around the harbour, out into Table Bay or, if you want to go further still, along the Atlantic seaboard for a sunset cruise to Clifton.

If you walk across the **Plaza** to the balustrade and look down to the lower level onto Victoria Basin's Quay (Quay 5), you'll see the quay operators' offices in what were once storerooms. Go down to the quay, and continue to **Quay 6** (East Pier Road), passing **Jetty 1** – at one time the embarkation point for prisoners en route to Robben Island – until you reach Jetty 2.

Alfresco Theatre

Just to the left, the glamorous **Table Bay Hotel**, recognisable by its distinctive green roof, and well-positioned for some of the best views in Cape Town, looks over the area. There's an entrance to the hotel from this side and a good bar for non-residents, as well as a restaurant at which you might want to take lunch. You can enjoy some pleasant moments sitting outside under the palms and admiring the view. Retrace your steps towards the Plaza area and continue to the **Amphitheatre**, which hosts concerts, alfresco theatre and other performances in the summer. It's wonderful when the wind isn't blowing, hell when it is. In this neighbourhood you'll find a wide variety

Above: the Waterfront mixes work and play

of inexpensive places to eat and places to sit in the sun.

Continue past the National Sea Rescue (one of six stations serving the region between Cape Point and Saldanha Bay), down towards the Victoria & Alfred Hotel and to the **Pierhead**, whose swing bridge takes you over 'the cut' to the **clocktower** area. Dominated by two fine port buildings, Pierhead is at the entrance to Alfred Basin. Look out for massive seals playing in the water here.

The clocktower itself, which was built in 1883, stands at the original entrance to the docks and was, before the docks' expansion, a signal station. Now, with its high-Victorian decorative style well-restored, it stands out like a deep ochre beacon. The **Old Port Captain's Building** that faces the clocktower from the other side of the cut is the Waterfront's administration centre. Temporary offices selling tickets for the boat trip to Robben Island *(see Excursion 2, page 49)* are situated next to the clocktower.

Return to Pierhead and continue west along the port side of the **Victoria & Alfred Hotel**, which occupies the site of warehouses once used by Union Castle mailships on their journeys to and from Cape Town. The hotel *(see Accommodation, page 82)* has a well-placed bar here, on a terrace facing the mountain and quite protected from the wind. This is an excellent place at which to have a drink while looking across the harbour to Table Mountain. Continue from the hotel and you come to the **Robinson Graving Dock** where ships are cleaned and repaired. The vessels are floated in, the gates are closed, and the dock is drained. The Waterfront's mix of working port and centre of commerce and entertainment is at its most apparent here.

If you continue further, you will cross the **bascule bridge** before finally arriving at the discreetly elegant **Cape Grace Hotel** *(see Accommodation, page 82)*, which has a good restaurant for lunch (or breakfast). If you can afford it, this first-class hotel is the place to stay. The open areas around the hotel, overlooked by the bridge, are destined for further development, with apartments and more shops due to be built.

Main Sights

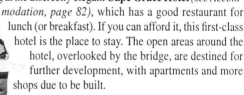

Retrace your steps and, after you have passed the Robinson Graving Dock, you enter an area that has some of the Waterfront's essential sights: the Two Oceans

Above: the clocktower
Left: Waterfront sounds

Aquarium, the Arts and Crafts Market housed in the Red Shed, and the South African Maritime Museum. You'll find a wealth of aquatic life, both freshwater and sea water, from around the Cape Peninsula at the **Two Oceans Aquarium** (daily 9.30am–6.30pm; tel: 021-418 3823; www.aquarium.co.za). It highlights the fragility of ecosystems, and of some of the country's marine life, and stresses the importance of preservation through dramatic displays. This is undoubtedly one of Cape Town's finest attractions. Huge tanks allow you to examine the specimens close-up. In particular, check out the Predators Tank for ragged-tooth sharks, short-tailed stingrays, turtles, yellowtails and shoals of a huge variety of local fish. The creatures swim around a towering forest of kelp and are kept healthy with a constant infusion of fresh sea water. You may want to take advantage of a scheme that allows visitors to don a wetsuit, dive into the tank and swim with the fish. Day or night-time dives are offered, but you'll need to book in advance and be in possession of a scuba licence.

Among the other aquarium attractions are a resident colony of Jackass penguins, a glass wall through which you can view the harbour's marine life (look out for the seals in particular) and a reconstruction of an ecosystem tracing a river's course from mountain top to sea. There's also an intertidal pool with mussels, barnacles, starfish and anemones and, in the same section, a child-friendly shallow pool where kids can touch starfish and the like under the supervision of staff.

Blowing Glass, Turning Pottery

Goods on sale at the **Arts and Crafts Market** (daily 9am–6pm) vary a lot in quality – some have a distinctly home-made feel – and its activities range from the fascinating to the fairly mundane. If you want to watch glass being blown and pottery being turned on a wheel, or you want to buy gifts made of leather or metal, this is the place. But for more interesting, up-market items such as African baskets, jewellery or fabulous printed textiles, try Victoria Wharf

The **South African Maritime Museum** (daily 10am–5pm; tel: 021-405 2880; www. museums.org.za/maritime) houses the SAS *Somerset* (the world's only extant boom defence vessel) and the *Alwyn Vincent*, built in 1959 and the only steam tug still in use in the southern hemisphere. It also has the country's largest collection of model ships.

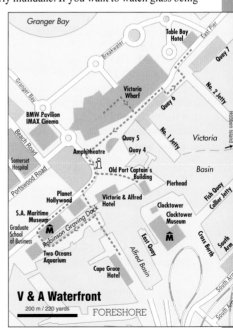

V & A Waterfront

200 m / 220 yards   FORESHORE

4. CAPE FLATS TOWNSHIPS *(see map, p38)*

You shouldn't visit townships unescorted, especially on your first trip.

A number of tour operators offer excursions: try Legend Tours (tel: 021-936 2814; www.legendtours.co.za) or Cape Care Route (tel: 021-426 4260; www.capecareroute.org.za).

The great majority of South Africans live in townships. It is a side to the country that few visitors, and indeed few white South Africans, ever explore. The townships were created in the apartheid years as 'independent homelands' in which blacks were forced to live. (To reside in 'white South Africa' blacks had to acquire work passes.) Cape Coloureds, who were not given a homeland, were granted employment in preference to blacks within the province. Large coloured settlements were established at Atlantis, north of Cape Town, and at Mitchell's Plain, on the False Bay coast. In 1984 the government made the black residential areas on the Cape Flats (Langa, Nyanga and Guguletu) available for coloured settlement.

   Meanwhile, the coloured suburb of District Six had been flattened in accordance with the Group Areas Act (1950), leaving an enormous scar where, since slaves were liberated in the1830s, a poor, gang-ridden but also vibrant community had lived on the slopes of Devil's Peak.

Triumph at Crossroads

The government wanted to reduce the number of blacks with residential rights and replace them with contract workers. Hence the destruction of the Cape Flats squatter camps in 1977–8, and the historic saga of Crossroads, a settlement close to Cape Town's main airport. It was at Crossroads that a

Above: a close society in a Cape Flats Township

progressive women's committee, supported by a large number of white sympathisers and considerable international publicity, encouraged the people to stand their ground despite the government's attempts at forceful removal. In 1981 the authorities finally allowed those with residential rights in the Cape Peninsula to stay – a triumph that galvanised resistance to apartheid. Crossroads grew rapidly, thereby creating further problems for officialdom.

By 1985 it was clear that the government intended to move the Crossroads community, together with all those in the black townships on the Cape Flats, to a new, controlled settlement on the False Bay Coast at Khayelitsha. In February of that year, as the police tried to demolish shacks, residents rioted; the government's brutal response left untold numbers shot, killed or maimed.

Khayelitsha

Khayelitsha is the Xhosa word for 'new home' but, for its million residents, it could easily mean 'early start'. The street lamps lighting Cape Town's white suburbs are still shining when Khayelitsha starts waking up. The township is, like Mitchell's Plain, near the ocean and is built on what were once sand dunes. During winter, when large parts of Khayelitsha are flooded, local newspapers frequently carry pictures of residents wading knee-deep, with buckets to scoop water out of their homes. Miles from the urban centre, it is today a mix of formal and informal settlements. The latter, mostly simple wood and iron shacks, are clearly visible from the main airport–town highway. According to a local saying, 'the rich get richer, the poor get Khayelitsha.'

Its crime statistics, especially for violent crimes such as murder and rape, are frightening, and unemployment hovers around 60 percent. Yet strangers are greeted warmly and neighbours tend to help each other out. Sidewalks are crowded with hawkers, and thriving *spaza* ('hidden' in township slang, in reference to the days when blacks were not permitted to run their own businesses) stores operate from private homes. These places sell a wide range of goods and services, from groceries to hairdressing and shoe repairs.

Despite their often lyrical names – Bishop Lavis, Steenberg, Hanover Park, Bonteheuwel, Manenberg, Elsies River, Langa ('sun'), Nyanga ('moon'), Gugulethu ('our pride') – the townships are dreary ghettos, which are often pervaded by a sense of hopelessness. Houses are usually tiny and overcrowded and in many areas endless apartment blocks serve as breeding grounds for gangsterism. The maintenance of buildings and roads is poor, though this is gradually being addressed.

However, for all their traumatic histories and pitiable conditions, the townships are energetic communal focal points with a feisty, inventive local culture that emphasises a sense of society and fellowship.

Right: neighbours help each other out

5. FROM MUSEUM TO MUSEUM *(see map, p22)*

A tour of Cape Town's museums can be done without leaving the city centre. Allow the best part of a day, depending on how long you would like to spend looking at the assorted exhibits.

Begin the walking tour at the Castle of Good Hope facing the Grand Parade (where there are lots of parking spaces).

The **Castle of Good Hope** (Mon–Sat 9am–5pm; tel: 021-469 1084), the oldest European building in South Africa, was constructed between 1666 and 1679 to defend the settlement from both the locals, and from possible attack by foreign navies. The castle, which replaced the simple square fortress erected by Jan van Riebeeck soon after his arrival in 1652, is pentagonal, in accordance with the military concept that protruding corner bastions give greater security. Hostile forces trying to breach the walls could be effectively resisted from the two nearest bastions. The design initially appeared in 16th-century Italy and was later perfected by the Dutch. This magnificent example was built with Robben Island stone and lime burnt from shells.

Today, where the garrison quarters, the deputy governor's house and the governor's residence – Simon van der Stel was the first governor to live here – used to stand, the castle precincts house a fascinating museum. The belltower above the town-facing entrance still has its original bell, cast in Amsterdam in 1697. Directly beneath it are the arms of the six Chambers of the East India Company and a broken pediment adorned by a crowned lion.

The Kat

Approach this beautiful structure across the moat and, passing a colonnaded walkway, enter the first courtyard, or bailey, through an immensely thick wall. The heart of the castle is divided into two sections: an outer and an inner bailey divided by a wall called the kat, against which a variety of official buildings once stood. Of these, the governor's residence sports the famous kat balcony which was added in the late 18th century and adorned with a high sculptured relief by Anton Anreith, who may have had his workshop in the castle at the time. The balcony was designed by either Anreith or Louis Michel Thibault. For a sharp contrast in living conditions, take a peek at the dungeons, in which criminals were locked away.

The governor's residence houses part of the William Fehr collections of Africana and early Cape antiques – consisting of furniture, textiles, silver and pictures – and includes masterpieces by Thomas Baines, a painter renowned for his depictions of life in the colony. Also well worth visiting is the castle's Military Museum, which exhibits displays of weaponry from the Dutch and British periods of occupation. There's so much to see at the castle that you might want to join one of its guided tours (hourly, 10am–3pm).

Left: Dutch East India Company private

Slave Lodge

In the colony's very early days, the building that now houses the **Cultural History Museum** (Mon-Fri 10am–4.30pm, Sat 10am–1pm; tel: 021-460 8200; www.museum.org.za) served as the Dutch East India Company's slave lodge. This is where the slaves slept, when they weren't being bought and sold under a tree in a neighbouring side street. The building was large enough to accommodate a kitchen, a hospital, a school and a gaol, but these facilities did little to improve the quality of the slaves' lives. Living conditions were appalling, and the death rate among inmates was particularly high. Badly ventilated in the summer, the place flooded during the winter.

When slavery was abolished in 1834, the building, now enlarged, was put to use as government offices. Its neoclassical appearance is the result of a Thibault makeover; the sculpture in the pediment on the Parliament Street side is Anreith's work. It later became the Old Supreme Court and finally a museum exhibiting wildly diverse displays of artefacts from sources ranging from the ancient Greeks to white South African immigrants.

Postal stones found in Table Bay form one of the most interesting exhibits in a section devoted to South African cultural history. Homesick mariners would leave messages inscribed with the name of the ship they were on under a large stone in the hope that fellow sailors, explorers, merchants or missionaries travelling in the other direction would deliver them home. The tombstones of van Riebeeck and his wife lie under the cobbled courtyard.

The **South African National Art Gallery** (10am–5pm except Mon; tel: 021-467 4660; www.museum.org.za) houses numerous rich collections, but today it's most famous for the contemporary art of the 'new' South Africa. See the Gainsboroughs and the Rembrandts if you want to, but you're probably better off heading for the art that is only now taking its place in the national and international cultural arenas after years of exclusion. There's 'township' art, 'protest' art and, ridding itself of historical baggage, 'South

Above: the Castle of Good Hope is the oldest European building in South Africa

African' art. Look out for the hybrid identity of two quite distinct cultures: the more formal, European-based aesthetic and, identifying with the continent's spirituality, the African tradition. Many of the gallery's pieces, by both black and white artists, fetch amazingly high prices internationally. The gallery also exhibits an excellent collection of southern African beadwork.

Bertram House, an annexe of the South African Cultural History Museum at the top of Government Avenue, is the home of the **British Colonial House Museum** Tues–Thurs 10am–4.30pm; tel: 021-481 3940). Here you can see how a well-to-do English family lived in the Cape in past centuries. The Regency-style rooms are resplendent with furniture, ceramics and silver; the building itself is a late Georgian affair faced with red bricks.

Prehistoric San Dioramas

The **South African Museum** (daily, 10am–5pm; tel: 021-481 3800; www.museum.org.za) dates back to 1897 and is the oldest in the country. This is the place to learn about southern African tribal culture. In addition to its attention-grabbing displays, which include dioramas of prehistoric San life, the museum has in storage collections of pots, baskets, spears, beadwork and jewellery, among other things, which can be viewed by special request.

In the public areas there's a collection of San rock art – if you can't get out into the country to see such works in situ, see them here. Also well worth seeing are sections on European furniture and *objets d'art*, dinosaur relics, and marine life from the oceans around South Africa. The museum is somewhat dated and in need of a makeover, but the displays make up for the cosmetic shortcomings. Part of the museum is given over to a planetarium (shows at 2pm Mon–Fri with extra show Tues 8pm; Sat shows noon, 1pm and 2.30pm; tel: 021-481 3900; www.museum.org.za) that looks at the southern hemisphere's night sky.

The **Old Town House**, also known as the Burgher Watch House (Mon–Fri 10am–5pm, Sat 10am–4pm; tel: 021-481 3933), is one of the country's loveliest buildings. Completed in 1761, it housed the burgher watch, the settlement's guard responsible for law and order and also for fire-fighting – in a settlement where highly inflammable thatch was the predominant roofing material. The house directly

Above and Left: at the South African Museum
Right: the South African Museum is the country's oldest

opposite Greenmarket Square replaced a simpler building that was demolished in the 1750s. Today, this gracious edifice, and its ponderous, mostly panelled interior, resembles a 17th-century Dutch guildhall. It's therefore quite appropriate that it contains the Michaelis collection of Dutch and Flemish paintings, donated by Max Michaelis. In a city that demolished more than 90 percent of its earliest buildings, it's worth noting that, the market din from the streets notwithstanding, the house's furniture, pictures, and even its smells, evoke another world.

Metropolitan life, such as it was in the early 18th century, is captured by the **Koopmans de Wet Museum** (Tues–Sat 9.30am–4.30pm; tel: 021-242473; www.museum.org.za). Housed in an 18th century town house at 35 Strand Street – once the town's most fashionable thoroughfare – it was built in 1701 by Reynier Smedinga, a silversmith, goldsmith, jeweller and enamellist, but much altered in about 1771. Check out the facade: it represents the fullest flowering of the neoclassical style in Cape Town, and has a simple pediment supported by four pilasters. It is one of the best-preserved buildings of its type in the city, although unfortunately now dwarfed by modern tower blocks.

Extravagant Trompe L'oeils

The house was acquired by the de Wet family at the beginning of the 19th century, and it remained their property until 1906 when Mrs Koopmans de Wet, a noted Cape Town personality, hostess and art collector, bequeathed it to the state as a museum. Today it features a collection of antiques, and walls adorned by extravagant trompe l'oeils.

Not far away, the **District Six Museum** (Mon–Sat 9am–4pm; tel: 021-461 8745; www.d6.co.za) at 25A Buitenkant Street, presents the other side of the coin: relics of a vibrant inner-city community destroyed during the apartheid era. At 71 Wale Street, the **Bo-Kaap Museum** *(see page 42)* portrays the lifestyle of a wealthy 19th-century Muslim family, complete with prayer room.

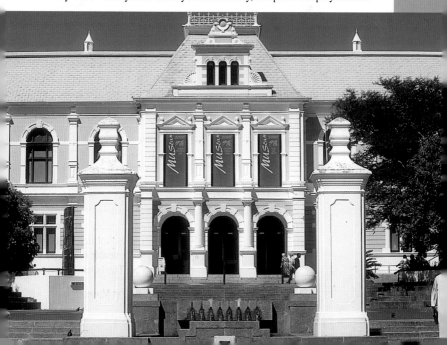

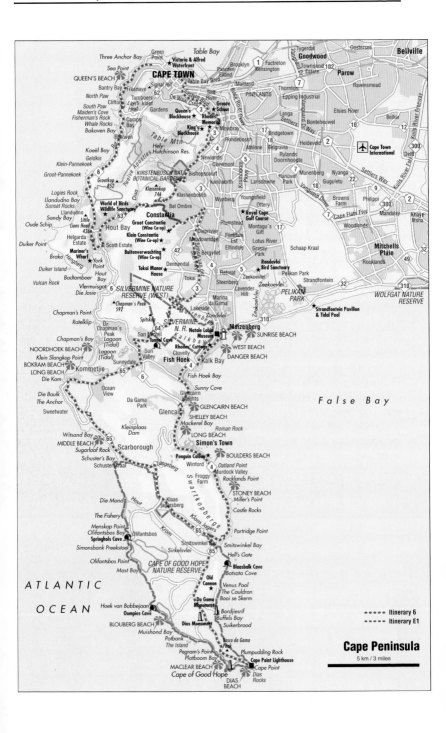

Cape Peninsula

5 km / 3 miles

- - - - Itinerary 6
- - - - Itinerary E1

6. THE SOUTHERN SUBURBS *(see maps, p 18–19 & 38)*

Set in the shadow of the mountain chain, the lush southern suburbs feature Cecil Rhodes's magnificent home, world-famous botanical gardens and a historic Cape Dutch wine estate.

This car trip takes a day from the city centre. Leave the city from the Fore-shore and climb the lower foothills using the Eastern Boulevard which, as De Waal Drive (N2), skirts the slopes of Devil's Peak, before becoming Rhodes Drive (M3). It continues around the base of the mountain, eventually reaching Groot Constantia.

The **Rhodes Memorial** edifice, a tribute by the architect Sir Herbert Baker to empire-builder Cecil Rhodes (1853–1902), was unveiled in 1912. Well-placed on the Groote Schuur part of Rhodes's Cape Town estate (which he bequeathed to the nation), it forms a strange U shape. Baker would locate his work in the most dramatic spots: the memorial overlooks the Southern Suburbs in their entirety. On a clear day you can see the sandy Cape Flats beyond the suburbs and the Hottentots Holland Mountains in the distance.

Built of Table Mountain granite, the memorial is a hefty classical-style building – in deference to Rhodes's standing as a scholar – approached by a ponderous series of stairwells. Look out for Swan's bust of the eminent colonialist, an inscription from Kipling's *The Burial*, and the bronze lions that pose at intervals on mighty stone plinths on the steps.

The focus of the memorial is George Frederick Watts's bronze horse, *Physical Energy*, which rears, nearly unbalancing its rider, at the base of the steps. Its name refers to Rhodes's prowess as a modern Renaissance man. Having seen the memorial, you could check out the estate's fallow deer – introduced by Rhodes himself – and other animals, such as wildebeest and zebra in the fields nearby. You can take tea or lunch (or indeed breakfast) in the Rhodes Memorial tearoom (daily 9am–5pm; tel: 021-689 9151).

Rhodes's Home

The estate's enormous **Groote Schuur** mansion was Rhodes's home. Originally a large barn, built in 1657 to store corn grown by the Dutch East India Company, it was acquired by Rhodes in 1893 and remodelled by Sir Herbert Baker shortly afterwards. One of Baker's first works in this country, its style harks back to the Cape Dutch. Though it eventually became the home of South Africa's state president, today it stands empty, its future undecided.

To visit Groote Schuur you need to get special permission (tel: 021-686 9100). Tours are limited to six per month, with places allocated on a first-come, first-served basis. Interior highlights include magnificent furniture, ceramic and textile

Right: Swan's bust of Rhodes

collections, and Rhodes's simple, almost schoolboyish bedroom.

Another part of Rhodes's estate that was bequeathed to the nation is the **Kirstenbosch National Botanical Gardens** (winter: 8am–6pm; summer: 8am–7pm; tel: 021-799 8899; www.nbi.ac.za). A 530-ha (1,300-acre) national treasure and home to one of the most important botanical collections in the world, Kirstenbosch stretches up to and includes the eastern flank of Table Mountain. There's plenty to do and see here *(see Excursion 2, page 25)*. You might choose to walk through the mountain *fynbos* (shrubs), or the formal gardens, which feature wonderful collections of flowers and trees. There's also a forest of cycads, a fragrance garden, a herb garden, rockeries, medicinal plants and a Braille trail for the blind.

Outdoor Concerts, Guided Walks

Plants on display includes ericas, pelargoniums, proteas and restios – you could see up to 6,000 of South Africa's 22,000 species. This is the place for indigenous flora, labelled and explained in publications sold at the estate's excellent bookshop (tel: 021-762 1621). If you're hungry, try the Fynbos (daily 9am–6pm) for breakfast and lunch or the Silver Tree (daily 11am–3pm, 6pm–10pm; tel: 021-762 9585) for lunch or dinner. You can buy plants and gifts in the Kirstenbosch Garden Centre (Mon–Sat 9am–6pm, Sun 9am–5pm; winter: 9am–5pm; tel: 021-797 1305). In summer the gardens host outdoor concerts – bring a picnic and a rug. The free Tuesday and Saturday guided walks (11am start; about 1½ hours' duration) are of the general-interest variety; there is a charge for the more specialised walk.

Governor Simon van der Stel, who planted the first vines in Constantia Valley, founded the **Groot Constantia** estate in 1685. The grand, gabled

homestead is a magnificent Cape Dutch building designed by Thibault. Carefully restored – the original burnt down in 1925 – it's a U-shaped building with a thatched roof and an impressive gable adorned by the figure of Abundance. Van der Stel took up residence at Groot Constantia in 1699, and he died there in 1712, having planted more than 8,000, mostly oak, trees. The estate was acquired by the Cloete family, in whose hands it remained until 1885, when it was sold to the state for use as an experimental vineyard.

Fine Wines and Furniture

The Cloetes made Groot Constantia's reputation. Under Hendrik Cloete, who enlarged the house and built the wine cellar in about 1791 – employing Anreith to decorate the pediment with a wine allegory now regarded as one of the country's finest works of sculpture – its wines became world-renowned. In its day (1778–1885) Constantia wines were imbibed by Napoleon and Nelson, and immortalised in literature by Jane Austen and Charles Dickens. The cellar is now a minor wine museum with a collection of early Cape furniture.

The house shows how a 17th- or 18th-century gentleman lived in the colony. Dark, heavy Dutch chests sit on terracotta floor tiles beneath Dutch seascapes, landscapes and still lifes. Among the textiles, silver and porcelain are antiques, many donated by the Dutch ship-owner Alfred de Pass.

Enter Groot Constantia from the car park through a small museum that traces the manor's history. You can see plans and samples of the building's original construction, and other artefacts. There's also a shop. Of the estate's two restaurants, Jonkershuis (9am until late except Sun and Mon evenings; tel: 021-794 6255) is housed in what was accommodation for the estate owner's bachelor sons. The food is homely, with an emphasis on Cape Malay cuisine. Drink Groot Constantia wines. The informal Tavern (10am–6pm; tel: 021-794 1144) serves lunch and teas; book for Friday or Saturday dinner.

Taste the wine (10am–5pm), and take a tour of the cellar (on the hour every hour except in winter when there are only two tours per day – this is, after all, a working farm). The reds are exceptional, particularly be sure to taste the Gouverneurs Reserve, and there is talk of reviving the fabled red Constantia muscats of the 18th century.

Having fallen into obscurity, the estate is now coming alive again. Located in the heart of the Cape's oldest viticultural area, it is part of the Constantia Wine Route, to which all of Groot Constantia's neighbours (especially Klein Constantia and Buitenverwachting) belong. Some of the Cape's best wines are produced here.

Kirstenbosch National Botanical Garden

250 m / 272 yards

Irrigation Dam (no entry) · Protea Garden · Protea Garden · Reservoir · Erica Garden · Seed Orchard · Cycad Amphitheatre · Colonel Bird's Bath · Director's House · Restio Garden · Pearson's Grave · Pelargonium Koppie · Education Centre · Matthew's Rockery · Herb Garden · Lecture Hall · Shop · Van Riebeeck's Hedge · Medicinal Plants · Fragrance Garden · Main Entrance · Rycroft Gate · Concert Stage · Mesem Banks (Vygies) · Main Pond · Clock · Restaurant · Annuals · Botanical Society · Peninsula Garden · Vlei Garden · Camphor Avenue · Nursery (no entry) · Curator's Office · Conservatory · Visitor's Centre · Pearson House · NBI Head Office · Rhodes Drive · Main Gate · Cape Town Rd · Wynberg · Kirstenbosch Stone Cottages

Above Left: at Kirstenbosch Gardens
Left: Groot Constantia

7. BO-KAAP (see map, p22)

A stroll through Bo-Kaap affords an uninterrupted view of old Cape Town, and insights into the local Cape Malay community.

This walk will take about 2 hours. Begin at the museum.

European settlers and freed slaves lived together in Bo-Kaap ('Above Cape Town'). As a result of its diverse cultures, the district has been known by a variety of names – The Malay Quarter, Signal Hill and, pejoratively, Slamse Buurt (*Slams* is a corruption of 'Islam'). The first Muslims arrived in the Cape as slaves, political exiles or prisoners from various parts of Asia and Africa. Drawn by the presence of coreligionists, Cape Muslims started arriving here in the 1830s. In 1952 Bo-Kaap was declared a Cape Muslim area under the notorious Group Areas Act; those who didn't fit that description were forced to leave. Today anyone has the right to live here, but the area is still

predominantly Muslim. Indeed the *muezzin* dawn call inviting the faithful to prayer is a familiar sound in the centre of Cape Town.

Begin this walking trour at the **Bo-Kaap Museum** (Mon–Sat 9.30am–4.30pm; tel: 021-481 3939; www.museum.org.za) occupying the district's oldest house (built in the 1760s, restored in the 1970s) which is still in its original cottage form. The facade's lovely baroque parapet and, on either side of the door, the sash windows' teak shutters, are typical of the early Cape Dutch house; the wide *voorstoep* and the design of the front door, with separate top and bottom panels, are distinctive features of local houses.

A Rare Relic

The neighbouring houses form a mix of later Cape Dutch and English Georgian styles. The cottage's fanlight (with window panes) is a rare relic of those traditions. There must have been lots of activity in the courtyard at the rear, originally shared by two households. The house exudes a Mediterranean feeling and is well suited to the hot climate.

The interior layout is very simple: four rooms and a central corridor leading to the courtyard. When it was built, by a Dutch settler, the neighbourhood was full of artisans; following the emancipation of slaves in 1834, many Muslims moved to the area, and the rooms you see here are much as they were when inhabited by a Muslim family in the 19th century. Most of the furniture is of the English, Dutch or types used at the Cape at the time. Only the kitchen appears as it might have in the late 18th century. The original hearth is intact and the floor is paved with Robben Island slate. For a guided tour, call Shireen Narkedien (tel: 021-422 1554).

Head down **Rose Street** to the **Bo-Kaap Bazaar** – the place to try some

Above: minaret of a mosque in the Bo-Kaap neighbourhood.
Above Right: an arresting residential exterior in Bo-Kaap. **Right:** a Cape Malay band

traditional Malay snacks (the Cape Muslims' culinary traditions are among the most ubiquitous of that community's many contributions to South African culture). Turn left into **Shortmarket Street** and you'll pass rows of traditional, often brightly painted, cottages. These are even quainter in the narrow, partially cobbled **Chiappini Street**, where each tiny house has a little *voorstoep* and sash windows: this is how old Cape Town looked. Turn right at Longmarket Street and you'll see, on the left, the **Pilgrim's Mosque**, the Masjid Koorhaanol Islam, with its onion-dome minaret. The mosque was built in 1886 and is virtually unchanged. Near the end of Chiappini Street is the **Shafi Mosque**, recognisable by its simple but distinctive minaret. In 1834 the Cape had two mosques, five Muslim prayer rooms and 12 Islamic schools, whereas, in the days of the Dutch, mosques were banned and Muslims had to worship in secret.

The Koran in Phonetic Afrikaans

In1797 the British allowed a freed prisoner, Tuan Guru (who had been expelled from Tidore in Indonesia and imprisoned on Robben Island) to open the **Auwal Mosque** in a Dorp Street warehouse. The building there today, enlarged and altered over the years, dates from 1809–1814. Tuan Guru became the leader of the Cape's Muslim community, and translated the Koran into phonetic Afrikaans at a time when this language was virtually unknown outside the slave community. The contribution of the Muslims to the development of the Afrikaans language is now widely recognised.

Excursions

1. THE CAPE OF GOOD HOPE NATURE RESERVE, THE CAPE PENINSULA *(see map, p38)*

A day-long car trip to The Cape of Good Hope Nature Reserve at the tip of the peninsula takes in a magnificent diversity of views. Pack beach gear, including a swimsuit, if you can face the sea's near-freezing water.

Start at Western Boulevard (M6) in Green Point, opposite the Green Point Stadium, follow Western Boulevard towards the sea and bear left onto Beach Road. In all, this route is about 160km (100 miles).

Beach Road, separating **Sea Point** from the sea, is a lovely promenade from which to watch the sunset and to begin a drive along the **Atlantic Seaboard**. Here, in Cape Town's version of Miami – Beach Road's Art Deco apartment blocks bask in the glow of dusk – joggers, nannies and speed-skaters are all out on the wide pavements. There are places to swim, but you're better off waiting until you reach the bigger, wider beaches further on. Sea Point is nowadays somewhat seedy, but if you happen to want a late-night meal, drink or dance, Main Road is the place to find a hive of activity all night long.

A Beach for the Beautiful

Clifton, reached after Bantry Bay, is the place to relax or take a dip. There are four coves: Fourth is for families; Third for body-building gays; Second for straight couples and gays; First is for anybody, but is largely used by residents of the immediate neighbourhood. Clifton is the beach of choice for gorgeous young Cape Tonians. Designer-label costumes are de rigueur, and you can hardly hear the crashing surf for the ringing of cellphones.

Only marginally less hectic is **Camps Bay**. The slopes above Camps Bay, Clifton and Bantry Bay comprise the country's most expensive real estate. The Camps Bay beach is wide and sandy, but very windy after noon, which is why, on a normal summer's day, you'll find it deserted after lunch. Facing the sea are a number of cafés and restaurants and one or two guesthouses and a hotel.

From Camps Bay to **Llandudno**, the drive along Victoria Road takes you past the peaks of the Twelve Apostles behind Table Mountain. This is a rare stretch of landscape, the only place near the city where mountain and sea are connected by undeveloped slopes. Llandudno has a sheltered beach for swimming and surfing, and nearby Sandy Bay's

Left: the Twelve Apostles overlook Clifton
Right: South Africa is now a 'rainbow nation'

glorious stretch of pristine sand is a haven for naturists. A walk of about a mile (nearly 2km) will get you there from the parking site (follow the signs from Llandudno). En route you pass a stretch devoted to gay men. Big, smooth rocks and small, hidden sunspots make this a delightful place in which to laze away the day. There are no shops in Llandudno or Sandy Bay, so if you intend spending the day, bring provisions, especially cool drinks.

Hout Bay

Between the Karbonkelberg and the last of the Apostles, the road leads to **Hout Bay**, formerly a wooded area that supplied the timber (*hout* is the Afrikaans word for 'wood') for Cape Town's buildings. Today Hout Bay is almost a suburb of the city, complete with plenty of little restaurants, bars and guest-houses. You could take a trip to the **World of Birds** (Valley Road, Hout Bay; daily 9am–6pm; tel: 021-790 2730) and walk through aviaries that contain up to 3,000 birds.

Or you might want to check out the **Hout Bay Museum**, a celebration of local history and industry (4 Andrews Road; Mon–Fri 8.30am–4.30pm, Sat 10am–4.30pm; tel: 021-790 3270). From Hout Bay, the route continues over Constantia Nek – follow the M63 and look out for the back of Table Mountain to the left – and down into Constantia (follow the M41), where it connects with the M3 freeway. The route sweeps over **Silvermine** and its nature reserve, and down towards **Noordhoek** and its lovely 6-km (4-mile) Long Beach, at which, incidentally, part of the movie *Ryan's Daughter* was shot.

At the furthermost end of Long Beach you will find the village of **Kommetjie**. Equestrian

Above: on the road to Noordhoek
Left: wild, virgin territory not far from the city

e x c u r s i o n s

types ride horses on the beach, surfers ride the waves and sunbathing families sprawl on the shore's Kommetjie end. Don't take to the water here – this stretch of ocean is very dangerous for swimmers. The road then skirts the mountains at the back of Kommetjie, passes **Scarborough**, a hamlet with a good restaurant and bar and a lovely, quiet beach for picnics, and heads on to the entrance to the **Cape of Good Hope Nature Reserve.**

The reserve encloses some 7,750 ha (19,000 acres) of wild, virgin territory, all covered with *fynbos*. This is the major vegetation type of the Cape Floral Kingdom, the smallest and, for its size, the richest of the world's six floral kingdoms. The nature reserve is one of the best places to see it – another is the Kirstenbosch National Botanical Garden, or you might consider a hike on Table Mountain itself. There are a number of good walks here, in particular the short distance to the tip of the peninsula. According to popular myth, the Atlantic and Indian oceans meet here; but this is not true. Wildlife on the reserve includes Cape mountain zebra , baboons, and a range of eland, bontebok, grey rhebok and grysbok. The reserve has a restaurant, and you can picnic on one of its lovely, remote beaches (Mon–Thurs 7.15am–4.30pm, Fri 7.15am–3.30pm; tel: 021-780 9204).

Swim with Penguins

Leaving the nature reserve, turn right and continue to Simonstown, passing en route **The Boulders**, a very pretty beach that is now home to a colony of rare jackass penguins. If you fancy a dip, you'll have to share the water with them. **Simonstown**, the next port of call, is the headquarters of South Africa's navy. There's plenty to see and do here and there are numerous restaurants and shops to tempt you to dawdle. The tourist information bureau is at 111 St George's Street (tel: 021-786 2436). The bay at Simonstown became a marine base in 1741 after vessels moored in Table Bay suffered a battering by winter storms. It was from here that the British invaded the Cape in 1795, wresting it from the Dutch to usher in a period now known as the First British Occupation. During World War II, Simonstown was a closed security area while its dockyard was devoted to repairing ships that had been damaged while protecting the Cape sea route. In 1957 the Royal Navy handed the dockyard to the South African navy.

Jubilee Square is at the hub of the town. Shops, restaurants and curio shops overlook the port, and there's a statue of Just Nuisance, the Great Dane that won the hearts of troops stationed here during the war. The dog was something of a mascot and even became formally enrolled in the Royal Navy as an able seaman.

The **Simonstown Museum** (Mon–Fri 9am–4pm, Sat 1pm–4pm; tel: 021-786 3046), housed in The Residency in Court Road, is worth a visit. Dating back to 1777, this could well be the town's oldest building.

Above: a colony of jackass penguins at The Boulders

Continuing around the coast, **Fish Hoek** has a lovely safe beach and is good for swimming, particularly for children, while **Kalk Bay** has Cape Town's longest stretch of pavement bric-a-brac and junk shops. **St James** was South Africa's favourite seaside destination at the turn of the 20th century – check out the many grand residences. One such mansion, at 192 Main Road, is now the **Natale Labia Museum** (Tues–Sun 10am–1pm, 2pm–5pm; tel: 021-788 4106; www.museums.org.za). Once the home of the then Italian Ambassador, Prince Natale Labia, and known as The Fort, it is now part of the South African National Gallery. It displays both permanent and temporary exhibitions and some of the main gallery's overflow.

The Simple Life for Rhodes

Also recommended to those interested in history is **Rhodes' Cottage**, Cecil Rhodes's holiday home, on the outskirts of Muizenberg. This simple, thatched building is at odds with the reputation of the immensely wealthy empire builder. **Muizenberg**'s tourist information bureau (52 Beach Road, tel: 021-788 6176; www.tourismcapetown.co.za) will supply you with details of historical walks in the area. Muizenberg has a magnificent beach with sands stretching for 40km (25 miles) all the way to Gordon's Bay on the other side of False Bay. Surfing is popular here, swimming is safe and the water warm. The area is rather shabby now, but a revival of this popular watering hole is on the cards.

2. ROBBEN ISLAND *(see map, p50)*

Visit the infamous former prison of Nelson Mandela.

Daily tours to Robben Island leave from Jetty 1 at the Victoria & Alfred Waterfront. For more information, call (021) 411 1006.

Few places in the world exemplify the struggle for basic human rights as **Robben Island** does. The presence of this prison island 11km (7 miles) north of Cape Town – where activists such as Nelson Mandela, Walter Sisulu, Govan Mbeki, Ahmed Kathrada, Robert Sobukwe and Neville Alexander were imprisoned for their opposition to apartheid – came to be seen by many as a symbol of the power to eradicate racism.

While attention has focused mainly on the island's role as a political prison, the 574-ha (1,400-acre) area has been put to a variety of uses, as a pantry, hospital, mental asylum and military camp. The early Dutch colonists saw the island as a larder; a place where they could hunt animals, grow crops and fatten livestock. At the time, Dutch colonialism was facing considerable resistance among the Muslim nations of East India and, closer to home, the Khoikhoi herders. Opposition leaders of both groups constituted the island's first prisoners. In fact, the island's first-known political prisoner was a local Khoikhoi leader, Autshumao, who was banished there in 1658 for alleged cattle theft.

When the British colonised the Cape in the 1800s they too used Robben Island as a prison. The legendary Xhosa prophet Nxele (also known as Makana) was imprisoned here in 1819 for leading an attack on Grahamstown. Makana drowned in a botched escape attempt, and consequently he became a figurehead of the opposition to colonialism. The island is sometimes referred to as the Island of Makana. Over time the island came to be used more as a hospital than a prison and by 1850 it housed large numbers of mentally ill and impoverished people as well as a huge colony of lepers, all living under the same harsh conditions as the prisoners before them. The 20th century brought change: by 1930, the lepers had been transferred to hospitals on the mainland and the population fell from a few thousand to a couple of lighthouse keepers. All the buildings were burnt to eliminate the infectious disease. In 1936, just before the outbreak of World War II, the island was occupied by the defence force for military purposes. It was used by the navy as a training centre in the 1950s, before the apartheid government decided in 1961 to once again turn Robben Island into a prison.

Between 1961 and 1991 more than 3,000 black male activists (legislation precluded females and whites from being jailed on the island) were held in the Robben Island prison, which was attracting international notoriety.

Top Left: family fun at the traditional resort of St James
Left: fishermen at busy Kalk Bay. **Above:** a watchtower at Robben Island

The last common-law prisoners – who were held separately from the political prisoners – left the island in September 1996.

Hard Labour

The island's limestone quarry was a place of hard labour for Nelson Mandela and his comrades, but it was also a place where the communication between prisoners led to the establishment of deep bonds and, ultimately, the triumph of the human spirit. An intense learning environment laid the foundations for tolerance and a future democratic culture in South Africa.

The **Robben Island Museum** (tel: 021-413 4200 or visit its website: www.robben-island.org.za) was established as a national monument in September 1996. Since January 1997, the island has been administered by the Department of Arts & Culture. On 1 December 1999, Robben Island was declared a World Heritage Site by UNESCO. The island is also an important nature reserve and home to a number of endangered species, particularly seabirds and jackass penguins.

The impact Robben Island has had on the lives of so many South Africans and the significance it continues to bear into the future is perhaps best described by Ahmed Kathrada, a former prisoner who now chairs the Future of Robben Island Committee:

'While we will not forget the brutality of apartheid, we will not want Robben Island to be a monument of our hardship and suffering. We would want it to be a monument reflecting the triumph of the human spirit against the forces of evil; the triumph of freedom and dignity over repression and humiliation; the triumph of wisdom and largess of spirit against small minds and pettiness; the triumph of courage and determination over human frailty and weakness; the triumph of non-racialism over bigotry and intolerance; the triumph of the new South Africa over the old.'

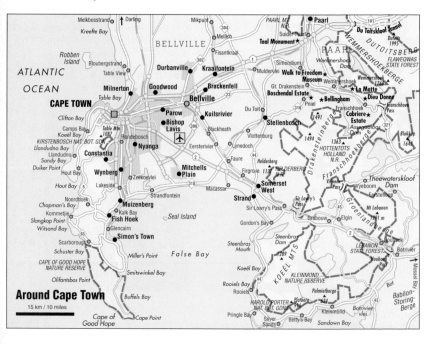

Around Cape Town

3. STELLENBOSCH *(see map, p53)*

A one-day walking tour of Stellenbosch, focusing on the town's history.

Begin the tour at the Tourist Information Bureau, 36 Mark Straat (Market Street; tel: 021-883 3584; www.stellenboschtourism.co.za), where you can pick up a map of the town centre. Continue east towards the VOC Kruithuis.

The first stop, **Rhenish Corner**, at the heart of old Stellenbosch is a complex of restored 19th-century buildings. These include the Cape Dutch **Rhenish Parsonage** (1815), which houses a museum of miniature rooms with period-style miniature furniture; **Leipoldt House** – a conglomeration of architectural styles, from Cape Dutch to English Georgian; and two modern education centres.

Continue to the **VOC Kruithuis** which, having served as the Dutch East India Company arsenal, is now a military museum with a minor collection of firearms. Built in 1777 opposite the Braak as part of the new settlement's fortifications, it has an unusual design. In a town prone to fires that often destroyed the thatched-roofed houses, this building is solid and fireproof. There's a barrel vault inside and, for extra protection, a high perimeter wall. Opposite the Kruithuis is the **Braak**, an open space of fallow land on which the burgher militia used to exercise. The Braak is comparable to a village green, and it's easy to imagine its role at the centre of the colonial townscape.

On the other side of the Braak, to the southeast, is the **Rhenish Mission Church**. Built in 1824, the church used to accommodate the crowds of 'slaves and heathens' who came to hear one Erasmus Smit, an enthusiastic missionary from Amsterdam. In 1829 the congregation was placed under the care of the Rhenish Missionary Society and in 1840, following the eman-

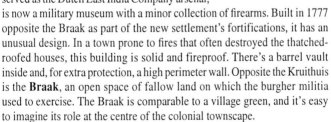

Top: the Hottentot-Holland Mountains
Right: the Rhenish Mission Church dates back to 1824

cipation of slaves, the church was enlarged. Look out for the magnificent carved pulpit that was a gift from the Moederkerk, and the lovely bells.

At 52 Ryneveld Street, the **Sasol Art Museum** houses a varied collection of anthropological artefacts and art from the university's collections. At No 18, you can see how Stellenbosch developed at the **Village Museum** (Mon–Sat 9.30am–5pm, Sun 2pm–5pm; tel: 021-887 2902). This complex comprises four separate buildings: Schreuder House, dating from 1709 and thus the oldest section, portrays the spartan lifestyle of the early settlers. Bletterman House (1798) and parts of Grosvenor House (*circa* 1803) depict life at the end of the 18th century and the early 1800s, while Bergh House, documenting life from the 1830 onwards, represents the home of a well-to-do family at the height of the Victorian era. Not that you have to visit a museum to get an idea of historic Stellenbosch: many of its cottages and houses, whether Cape Dutch, English Georgian, Regency or Victorian, are original.

Next door is the **Moederkerk**. This neo-Gothic Dutch Reformed Church was rebuilt at various stages in the 19th century, replacing the building on which construction began at the beginning of the 18th century. The spire was completed in 1866. Next to the Moederkerk, at the junction of Ryneveld Street and Dorp Street is **Church House**, built between 1753 and 1787. Opposite Church House, the **Theological Seminary** occupies arguably the most historic site in town.

Here, on the original island formed by the Eerste River, the earliest settlers, including Simon van der Stel – the first governor, after whom Stellenbosch (Stel's forest) was named – staked their claim to the land. Governor van der Stel planted some of the oaks for which Stellenbosch is now famous.

The oak-lined **Dorp Street**, a former wagon road with some original, well-preserved facades, gives a good idea of what the early town looked like. Probably no other street in the country has as much historical architecture as Dorp Street which, along with Church Street and Van Ryneveld Street, is one of the oldest in the town centre. The Eerste River to the south runs parallel. The houses on the river side of the street once had long gardens stretching down to the river bank. The original houses on the town side were single-storied, although many later acquired an upper level.

Street highlights include the **Oude Leeskamer** – the Old Reading Room at No 182 with its very simple, mid-

Above: Boschendal vineyard
Right: Oom Samie se Winkel

19th century gable; **Saxenhof**, at No 159 – an 18th-century house with 19th-century modifications, that was once home to the first South African-trained doctor, Jacob Versveld; and, most importantly, at No 116, **Voorgelegen**. This H-shaped house was built around 1798 and was once gabled in the manner of **La Gratitude**, at No 95 across the road. This lovely building is a restoration of an 18th-century homestead that was destroyed by fire in 1803, and again in the 20th century. Its gable is adorned by the eye of the Almighty – an eye in a bas relief surrounded by rays. At 84–82,**Oom Samie se Winkel** (daily 8am–5.30pm; tel: 021-887 0797) is a good example of a former trading store of the type once found in any South African country town. Today it's a tourist attraction filled with bric-a-brac and expensive junk.

The Rembrandt Collection

The Cape Dutch, H-shaped homestead **Klein Libertas** (Mon–Fri 9am–noon, 2–5pm, Sat 10am–1pm, 2–5pm; tel: 021-809 7473), also known as Libertas Parva, at 33–25, dates from 1783, and houses the Rembrandt tobacco corporation's collection of South African paintings. It is well worth visiting this exhibition as it includes works by Irma Stern and William Kentridge and sculptors of Anton van Wouw's calibre.

In the cellar at the back is the **Stellenryk Wine Museum** (Mon–Fri 9am–12.45pm, 2–5pm, Sat 10am–1pm 2–5pm; tel: 021-888 3588; www.museums.org.za). Stellenbosch lies at the centre of the country's oldest wine-making district after the Constantia Valley in Cape Town. Overlooked by the Hottentots Holland, the Helderberg, the Stellenbosch and the Simonsberg mountain ranges, the valley is famously fertile.Return to Market Street and then into **Herte Street** to see, at No 25–35, a row of semi-detached houses built for liberated slaves in the mid-19th century by the Rhenish Mission Society.

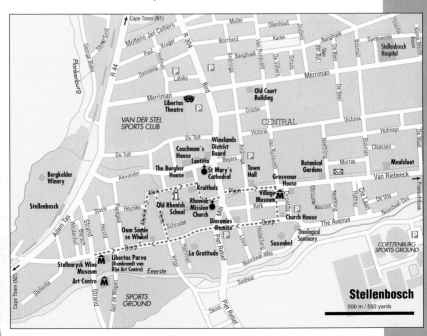

4. THE FRANSCHHOEK WINE ROUTE *(see map, p50)*

A driving tour of the wine estates in the Franschhoek Valley, with plenty of opportunities to taste the fruits of South African viticulture.

Follow the N1 from Cape Town and, at Exit 47 (to Wellington) branch left and turn immediately right. Continue over the first intersection, turn left; then continue to the intersection with the R45. Turn right and continue on to Franschhoek (about 19km/11 miles).

Franschhoek is a small country town some 60km (37 miles) from Cape Town. It lies at the heart of the Cape winelands, in a small valley where elephants once roamed in great numbers. Nowadays the Franschhoek Valley, hemmed in by the Franshhoek and Groot Drakenstein mountains, is more famous for its vineyards and its French connection. Franschhoek's wine route is small compared to those of Stellenbosch and Paarl, but it does produce some excellent results, and the town of Franshhoek itself has some fine restaurants, hotels and guesthouses. For a vineyard visit with a specialist tour operator, try Vineyard Ventures (tel: 021-434 8888; www.vineyardventures.co.za).

While in the area you may also want to visit the new 'Walk to Freedom' museum – the prison bungalow in which Nelson Mandela spent the last 18 months of his imprisonment. The bungalow, described by Mandela as his gilded cage, sits in the Groot Drakenstein Prison (previously called Victor Verster Prison), just outside Paarl on the R301 road towards Franschhoek (tel: 021-872 3829 for opening hours).

Porcelain and Period Furniture

A farm worth visiting is **Boschendal**, just off the R45 at its junction with the R310. Not only is it an historic estate with a well-restored H-plan Cape Dutch house (built in 1685, rebuilt in its present form in 1812), but it also produces excellent wine, and has a good range of lunch options. Governor van der Stel originally granted the estate to the French Huguenot Jean le Long, and eventually it was acquired by the de Villiers family.

Today it is owned by Rhodes Fruit Farms and the house is no longer a private home. Open to the public (Mon–Fri 9am–5pm; also Sat, Sun 10am–12.30pm in Dec/Jan; tel: 021-870 4281; www.boschendal.com), it contains a splendid collection of porcelain and period furniture, just as it might have done 150 years ago. The Boschendal Restaurant, featuring hot and cold buffets and fine local cheeses, is open daily for lunch but book in advance (tel: 021-870 4274).

Le Café (daily 8.30am–4.30pm; tel: 021 870 4283) serves lighter meals and teas, while Le Pique-Nique (Nov–Apr daily; booking essential; tel: 021-870 4274) is for alfresco meals in the gardens – weather permitting.

Back on the R45, the route continues to **L'Ormarins** (weekdays 9am–4.30pm, Sat 9am–12.30pm; tel: 021-874 1026; www.lormarins.co.za). The wine at L'Ormarins is excellent. The estate belongs to the South African Rupert family that owns Chanel and other luxury labels. Unfortunately the site's Cape Dutch homestead (built in 1811) is not open to the public, but it can be glimpsed beyond a lovely garden that you pass on the approach to the cellars.

You can follow this with a visit to another estate – **Bellingham** (Dec–Jan Mon–Sat 11am–4pm; tel: 021-874 1011; www.bellingham.co.za), an historic property graced by a lovely H-plan homestead with an 18th-century gable. At Bellingham you can enjoy a light alfresco lunch washed down with farm wines. Wine tastings are available (Nov–Apr: Mon–Fri 9am–5pm, Sat 10am–12.30pm; May–Oct: Mon–Fri 9am–4.30pm; tel: 021-984 1011). This is the property on which the Cape's first Premier Grand Cru dry white blend was produced, and also the first shiraz.

Further on is **La Motte** (Mon–Fri 9am–4.30pm, Sat 9am–noon; cellar tours by appointment only; tel: 021-876 3114; www.la-motte.com), another Rupert property set on another 17th-century estate. La Motte is known for its shiraz and for Millennium, its flagship Bordeaux-style red.

Cabernet Sauvignon in Happy Valley

Also delightful is **Moreson** (Dec–Apr: Wed–Sun 11am–5pm; May–Nov: Tues–Sun 11am–3pm; tel: 021-876 3055; www.moreson.co.za), sometimes referred to as Moreson-Matin Soleil. Turn right off the R45 and into Happy Valley Road for an estate that has excellent whites and, notably, a cabernet sauvignon '95 that alone is worth stopping for. You could have a light lunch here at the Moreson Bread & Wine restaurant (tel: 021 876 3692), which features a Mediterranean-style menu. Booking is essential for this relaxed, informal estate.

Connoisseurs will appreciate **Rickety Bridge** (daily, Nov–May: 10.30am–5pm; June–Oct: 11am–4.30pm; cellar

Left: a winery's produce stored for local consumption or export
Above: local labourers after a hard day's work

tours by appointment; tel: 021-876 2129; www.ricketybridgewinery.com), another historic property whose sauvignon blanc '97 and Chenin Blanc '96 and '97 are especially recommended. It's open for tastings and sales.

Next on the route is **Grand Provence Farm**, which is owned by an Italian count who amalgamated the Haute Provence and La Provence farms. The latter has one of the Cape's best-preserved early homesteads, dating back to the second half of the 18th century. The wines at Grand Provence are first class. Taste them over lunch at Le Provençal restaurant, which you'll find in an early Cape barn deep in the vineyards. A local speciality, Franschhoek trout, is served in four ways here. The wine lists feature only Franschhoek wines: if you can't make the whole tour, try the local vintages here with your lunch.

Turn left up Uitkyk Road and not far away, **Chamonix Wine Farm** (www.chamonix.co.za) presents an alternative option for lunch with a French-inspired menu (lunch daily, dinner Fri, Sat; tel: 021-876 2494). Before lunch you can sample wines from the farm in the adjoining underground cellar.

Further up the Uitkyk Road you can visit the cellar and taste the excellent cabernet sauvignon and chardonnay at the **Dieu Donne** vineyards. (weekdays 9.30am–4.30pm; in summer also Sat, Sun 9.30am–12.30pm; tel: 021-876 2493; www.dieudonnevineyards.com). Unlike many of area's wineries, Dieu Donne produces its own wines rather than having them made at the local co-operative.

Cabriere Estate is the next stop on this wine route. The estate is known for

its pinot noir and chardonnay grapes, from which its quite famous brandy and sparkling and fortified wines are made. As well as wine tastings (Mon–Sat, 11am and 3pm), and sales (Mon–Sat 9am–4.30pm), it arranges cellar tours by appointment (tel: 021-876 2630; www.cabriere.co.za). The Saturday tour, conducted by the owner Baron Achim von Arnim, is hugely entertaining and very informative.

Franschhoek Town

A number of other vineyards in and around the town are worth visiting if you have time and the inclination. Should you decide to spend a weekend in Franschhoek (*see Accommodation, page 87*), you can pick up relevant details at the **tourist information office** (tel: 021-876 3603; www.franschhoek.org.za) in the main street just as you enter the town.

Top Right: the Huguenot monument.
Above: the Franschhoek Winery, where you will find local wines. **Right:** inside the museum

Beyond the attractions of wine, food appreciation is a big deal here. You can't go wrong if you choose between Le Quartier Francais (16–18 Huguenot Street; tel: 021-876 2151; www.lqf.co.za; breakfasts, lunches, teas and dinners daily), La Petite Ferme (lunch daily; tel: 021-876 3016) on the Franschhoek Pass just beyond the town – turn left at the Huguenot Memorial and Haute Cabriere Cellar Restaurant (daily for lunch, Fri–Sat for dinner in the summer; tel: 021-876 3688), also on the Franschhoek Pass. The decor shop **La Grange** has a café serving light lunches and offering lovely views.

Bastille Day

There are lots of places to shop for homeware accessories, antiques and bric-a-brac, and the walks and drives in and around the area are diverting enough for a weekend's touring. If you intend visiting on Bastille Day (14 July) be sure to book accommodation and make a restaurant reservation well in advance. For this French holiday, the entire town grinds to a halt and there's a small, popular village-like fête. The ubiquitous French presence dates back to the 17th century. In 1685, Louis XIV revoked the Edict of Nantes to deny civil rights to Huguenots (Protestants) who thus fled abroad. The names of many farms – La Bourgogne, La Provence, L'Ormarins – hint at their original owners' provenance. The Huguenots introduced most of the viticultural traditions that are still followed by many families.

The **French Huguenot Museum** (Mon–Sat 9am–5pm, Sun 2pm–5pm; tel: 021-876 2532; www.museum.co.za) and monument is at the end of the main street that bisects the town, in Lambrecht Street. The museum has 18th-century furniture, paintings and memorabilia, and a research facility for the descendants of Huguenot families, many of whose surnames (such as du Toit, Malherbe, de Villiers) are still common. The museum building is a replica of an 18th-century town house called Saasveld that once stood in the Gardens area of Cape Town. The town house was demolished during the 1950s but some of its contents reappeared here. Designed by Thibault, it shows the quality of early Cape architecture.

5. DARLING AND THE WEST COAST NATIONAL PARK
(see pull-out map)

This round trip via Darling can easily be done by car in a day.

The route begins on the N1, at the Paarden Eiland turnoff to the R27, which heads up the west coast. It travels through Milnerton and Tableview before heading through a precious wilderness which, in season, is aglow with daisies and flowering succulents. Some 85km (50 miles) from the N1 turnoff, branch right at the R315 crossing and head for Darling.

The best time of the year to enjoy this excursion is early spring, when the wild flowers form an awesome display. If you don't have time to explore the region, Darling itself, known as the west coast's 'flower village', gives a good idea of the surrounding area's beauty. The town's floral wealth derives largely from a wide range of bulbous plants and other perennials that pop up each spring, producing blooms you would be hard-pressed to find anywhere else in the world. The flowers generally blossom from August to October, and bear in mind that they open only on sunny days. Drive with the sun behind you, so that the flowers face you. Check the weather conditions before you go.

Darling is surrounded by dairy farms, wheat fields and vineyards. This part of the country is more English shire than Cape veld, and only the occasional Cape Dutch farmhouse reminds you that you're in South Africa. This little town, with its sprinkling of Victorian villas and its rigid,

Top: the West Coast National Park
Left: tables await at Evita se Perron

gridlike town plan, is famous for its wild-flower and orchid shows, held every 14–17 September, which always attract large crowds.

There are a number of attractions in Darling, and a choice of lunch venues. The **Darling Museum and Information Centre** (corner Pastorie and Hill streets; Mon–Fri 9am–1pm, 2–4pm, weekends 10am–1pm, 2–4pm; tel: 022-492 3361) is a typical village museum. Focusing on local heritage, it looks at the town's history as a major producer of butter. The Darling Creamery was founded in 1902, and the butter it produced was a mainstay in the lives of many South Africans until the 1960s.

Political Satire

Evita se Perron ('Evita's Platform') is an informal theatre venue at old Darling Railway Station (follow the signs) that specialises in political satire, in particular the work of Pieter-Dirk Uys, much of it delivered by his alter ego, Evita Bezuidenhout. Make reservations for these hilarious performances, accompanied by dinner and drinks (Lunch: Sat, Sun; dinner: Fri, Sat; light meals: Mon–Fri 10am–3pm; tel: 022-492 2851; www.evita.co.za).

Between Darling and the sea on the R315, you'll find **Tienie Versveld Flower Reserve** (tel: 021-762 1166). Admission is free to this sectioned-off piece of a farm whose landscape is unsullied by animals or humans. Drive in, but stick to the tracks, to see the wild flowers, such as vygies, that grow in profusion here. In season, look out for informal signs to other farms, such as Waylands and Oudepost, that are open to the public (call the information centre at the museum for details). Oudepost, the biggest orchid nursery in South Africa, exports millions of exotic blooms overseas every year.

If you want to taste the local wine, head for Mamreweg, a few kilometres inland from Darling, and the **Darling Cellars** (Mon–Thurs 9am–5pm, Fri 9am–4pm, Sat 9am–noon; tel: 022-492 2276; www.darlingcellars.co.za), where there are tastings and sales. Look out for some wonderful sauvignon blanc.

From Darling head back to the R27, continue right, in the direction of Langebaan, but branch off the highway at the signs to the **West Coast National Park** (winter 7am–7.30pm; summer 6am–8pm; tel: 022-772 2144/5; www.parks-sa.co.za). This lovely area includes the Langebaan Lagoon (in which you can swim), the Saldanha Bay islands of Schaapen, Jutten, Marcus and Malgas, and the little **Postberg Nature Reserve** (Aug–Sept daily 9am–4pm). At this, one of the prettiest spots on the coast, you might want to stop in the village of Churchhaven, where you can park and swim. More than 25 million water birds (ibis, pelican, heron and others) in addition to eland, kudu and zebra, subsist here, in one of the world's most important wetlands. For further information about the area, call the Geelbek Education Centre (tel: 022-772 2798). Return to Cape Town on the R27.

Right: spring blooms

Leisure
Activities

SHOPPING

Compared with European and American cities, Cape Town doesn't have a great variety of shops, and this certainly isn't the place to buy designer labels. But for the work of local craftsmen, especially ceramics, basketware and beadwork, it's second to none. These days foreign visitors are buying more and more home accessories from the city's decor and design shops. Meanwhile South African furniture and fabrics are showcased in the fashionable salons of London, New York and Paris.

Animal Products

Be very careful about buying animal products. Never be tempted to buy ivory, not least because you will be unable to import items into your own country. But plenty of intriguing animal products – those made from the bones or hides of culled animals, ostrich eggs, and leather products such as wallets, handbags, belts and shoes – can be bought. **African Light & Trading** (31 Wesley Street, Gardens; tel: 021-462 1490) has a fine selection of homeware and furniture. Check out the lighting fixtures that incorporate ostrich eggs. Hides (zebra and springbok are the most widely available) are popular with visitors, but for export purposes, each item must be docketed (that is, it must come from a culled beast).

Antiques

South Africa's best antiques shops are in Cape Town and Johannesburg. Don't expect to find rare masterpieces, the finest silver, or museum-quality furniture here, precious little of which ever made it to South Africa in the first place. What you will find is lots of 19th-century furniture – Persian carpets, Art Deco lamps, mirrors, decorative objects and, increasingly, an eclectic array of French provincial furniture, all of it recently imported, particularly in the wake of the fashion for all things Provençale. Foreigners have been

known to buy such items and ship them home, so good are the prices and so favourable the exchange rate.

There is a series of antiques, bric-a-brac and junk shops in and around **Church Street**, at the upper end of **Long Street**. For first-class antiques, try **Le Brocanteur** (Shop 3A, Gardens Centre, Mill Street, Gardens; tel: 021-461 6805) which sells French cupboards and other pieces of furniture, silver and tableware. **Bygones Antiques & Summerhouse** (8 Augusta Way, Constantia 7800; tel: 021-794 5489) stocks a variety of French and English furniture, ceramics and silver as well as contemporary bed linen, china and glass. The shops on the Main Road in **Kalk Bay**, opposite the railway station, are also worth visiting for bric-a-brac and junk. You'll find all kinds of things spilling out onto the pavement. This area is also good for cafés, gift shops and a variety of odd emporia that deal in everything from printed fabric to wire baskets and elephant skulls.

Serious collectors might be attracted by genuine, and often rare, South African antiques – such as early Cape furniture (chests, cupboards, dining chairs and tables and the like) and objects made from silver and pewter – but they don't come cheap. Cape Town's finest quality pieces can be found at **Deon Viljoen** (1 Palmboom Road, Newlands 7700; tel: 021-686 4344; www.deonviljoen.com) and

Left: Church Street bric-a-brac
Right: local fabrics

Michael Stevenson (which is also at 1 Palm-boom Road, Newlands 7700; tel: 021-685 2220; www.michaelstevenson.com).

In Stellenbosch **Pier Rabe Antiques** (141-143 Dorp Street, Stellenbosch 7600; tel: 021-883 9730) is definitely the best place. The decorative and fine arts auctioneers **Ashbey's Galleries** (43 Church Street; tel: 021-423 8060) hold weekly sales of art and antiques.

Arts, Crafts & Curios

Two of the city's best curio shops are **African Image** (corner of Burg and Church streets; tel: 021-423 8385; www.african-image.co.za) and **The Collector** (52 Church Street; tel: 021-423 1483) are good for locally made baskets, beadwork and ceramics, and, from elsewhere in Africa, textiles, sculpture and jewellery. When considering a purchase, ask about the item's provenance. Old (antique) South African beadwork is very rare, and what you'll be offered, while pretty or enchanting, is probably not more than 20 years old. San (Bushman) curios are even rarer.

If you're not in the market for antiquities, look out for sculpture, baskets, torchères, chandeliers and the like. Local craftsmen use a diverse range of materials, including twisted wire, painted fabrics, traditional clay pots, wooden bowls, spoons and plates. If buying such craftwork at Sunday's **Green Point Market**, which is a very good source,

be sure to haggle over prices. The Green-market Square market has a less varied range of goods, and the prices tend to be fixed.

Books & Maps
Bookshops

One of the best bookshop chains is Exclusive Books, which has 9 outlets in Western Cape, including at the Victoria & Alfred Water-front (tel: 021-419 0905), Constantia Village Shopping Centre (tel: 021-794 7800) and Cavendish Square (tel: 021-674 3030), an upmarket shopping mall in the suburb of Claremont; www.exclusivebooks.com. The chain sells newspapers and magazines, maps, guidebooks, novels and coffee-table volumes.

CNA (Central News Agency) is a newsagent chain that sells stationery as well as magazines and newspapers. CNA isn't big on novels and coffee-table, but you will find guidebooks and maps. Two highly recommended branches are at: Victoria & Alfred Waterfront (tel: 021-418 3510) and Constantia Village Shopping Centre (tel: 021-794 5835).

Antiquarian books and maps are rather thin on the ground but you could try Michael Stevenson *(see Antiques above)* or **Clarke's Bookshop** (211 Long Street, Cape Town 8001; tel: 021-423 5739; www.clarkes-books.co.za). Most bookshops sell tourist maps and guides. There are plenty of second-hand bookshops at the upper end of **Long Street** in the city centre. This is the place to browse for that long-remaindered edition of your favourite book.

Decor & Design

The world of South African decor and design is a good reflection of both the locals' crafts skills and the country's melting-pot culture. In other words, the Africa motif evident in animal products, textured fabrics, earth colours and suchlike has been married to a Western sensibility to produce sophisticated products. For the first time, South African craftsmen are responding to the materials around them in new and interesting ways.

To see the results, pay a visit to **African Light & Trading** (31 Wesley Street, Gardens; tel: 021-462 1490) for leather furniture and accessories made of horn or bone; **Okha** (186 Loop Street, Cape Town 8001; tel: 021-

Above: authentic African masks make great souvenirs
Right: Long Street is the place for curios

424 9706; www.okha.co.za) for fabrics, furniture, lighting and ceramics, all so chic you'll think you've died and gone to Paris; **Colonial House** (80 Long Street, Cape Town; tel: 021-424 7355), for basket-weave furniture, storm lanterns and other items reminiscent of colonial Africa; **Block & Chisel Interiors** (207–209 Main Road, Diep River; tel: 021-712 5193) for Asian furniture and accessories; and **LIM** (86A Kloof Street, Tamboerskloof, Cape Town 8001; tel: 021-423 1200) for pared-down, often stark furniture and accessories.

One of the finest crafts stores is out in Franschhoek: **La Grange** (13 Daniel Hugo Street, Franschhoek 7690; tel: 021-876 2155) stocks locally made ceramics in the latest colours, South African art, Indian pewter, local raffia and rattan products, furniture, glassware and more.

Food & Wine

Which food and drink items will you want to take home? Most wine buffs will want to take samples from the Cape Winelands which, in addition to their quality, are easy to find, and taste. You can buy direct from the individual estates – always a good idea after a wine-tasting tour.

Although many of South Africa's mainstream labels are these days available in Europe and America, bear in mind that specialist and estate wines may not be. One of the best specialist outlets for quality wine is **Vaughn Johnson** (adjacent to Planet Hollywood, Victoria & Alfred Waterfront; tel: 021-419 2121).

Shipping wines to your home country is easy to arrange, but not cheap, so, before you decide to ship it is sensible to check that you can't buy your purchases in your home country. The merchant or estate should be able to advise you. Local port and sherry are also attractive buys, as is grappa from the Meerlust estate.

Food products that you're less likely to find easily at home include *konfyt* (fruit preserved in sugar and bottled in jars), unusual dried fruit and, individual stomachs permitting, tinned crocodile or venison pâté. You should be able to find *konfyt* and dried fruit at any supermarket (you will find **Pick & Pay** supermarkets everywhere) or delicatessen – try **Giovanni's** (Main Road, Green Point; tel: 021-434 6893), which is also good for game pâté, or **Melissa's** (94 Kloof Street, Tamboerskloof, Cape Town 8001; tel: 021-424 5540), which also sells groceries such as local cheeses, olive oils, biscuits and chocolates.

Jewellery, Gems & Minerals

The city's best jeweller is **Charles Greig** (Upper Level, 3rd Entrance, Victoria & Alfred Waterfront; tel: 418 4517). Here you will find what seems like all the gems of

Africa – dazzling diamonds, emeralds, tourmaline, topaz and amethyst. You will find many other jewellers scattered throughout the city, but in particular, check out St George's Mall, Cavendish Square Shopping Centre (enter at Cavendish Street, Claremont 7700; tel: 021-674 3050), or the Gardens Centre (Mill Street, Gardens, Cape Town 8001; tel: 021-465 1842).

At a slightly less exalted level, attractive gemstone necklaces, cuff links, bracelets and rings are widely available. For raw chunks

of minerals and gemstone, you might like to try the **Scratch Patch** chain, particularly the Simonstown outlet (Dido Valley Road, Simonstown; tel: 021- 786 2020).

Markets

Cape Town's two main markets are the daily flea market held in **Greenmarket Square** (clothes, jewellery, second-hand books, shoes and curios) in the city centre, and a Sunday market at **Green Point Stadium** (as above plus food, bric-a-brac, plants and second-hand furniture) on Fritz Sonnenberg Road, not far from the Victoria & Alfred Waterfront. You will find plenty of coffee shops and restaurants, but almost no park-

ing, at the former; haggling over prices and lots of parking at the latter.

Paintings

South African paintings, in particular the work of Irma Stern, are currently fetching high prices in Europe. If you don't have up to a million rand to spend on a picture but want to acquaint yourself with the country's contemporary art scene, you should visit **Joao Ferreira Fine Art** (80 Hout Street, Cape Town 8001; tel: 021-423 5403; www.joaoferreiragallery.com), where the work tends towards avant-garde, and the **Everard Read Gallery** (3 Portswood Road, Victoria & Alfred Waterfront; tel: 021-418 4527; www.everardread.co.za), the city's most serious fine-art dealer, which has a sister gallery in Johannesburg. Their prices are high but the changing exhibitions provide a comprehensive view of what's going on in the South African art market.

Ceramics

In the world of ceramics there is a wide variety of products, including a lot of rubbish, so if you want to buy serious work it is essential to go to a reputable dealer. **The Peter Visser Gallery** (68 Church Street, Cape Town 8001; tel: 021-423 7485), which specialises in young and upcoming artists, but not at the expense of one or two established names, is a good place to go. Among South Africa's many ceramicists, the work of Hylton Nel is fetching astronomical prices at The Fine Art Society in London's Bond Street.

Shells

Shells are hard to find, even on the beaches. But you should be able to buy sme pretty examples, particularly from Mauritius, at Green Point Market on Sunday mornings (from about 9.30am).

If you want to collect interesting shells fresh from the ocean your best bet is best to travel north of Cape Town to Jeffrey's Bay in the Eastern Cape. You will often see Perlemoen shells used as ashtrays or hors d'oeuvre dishes in Cape Town homes and restaurants.

Don't be tempted to buy coral: anything offered to you probably comes from rare stocks in endangered coral fields, and shouldn't be touched.

Above: a new twist on metalwork

EATING OUT

Cape Town is easily South Africa's most cosmopolitan city. Like many of the world's ports, it has traditionally provided food and lodgings to seafarers, and attracted a wide variety of wanderers, from imperialists and missionaries to refugees, fortune-seekers and remittance men (those living abroad on money sent from home – a phenomenon common in the days of the British empire).

Nowadays, as the new South Africa attracts more and more foreign visitors, and as increasing numbers of locals travel abroad, the array of culinary styles has grown to the extent that you are as likely to find first-class French provincial cooking here as you are to stumble upon Chinese, Cajun or Californian dishes. There are four staples to South Africa's culinary culture:

● The Afrikaaner tradition consists largely of the food eaten by the early Dutch colonists with French Huguenot and German-settler influences: in other words, heavy meat dishes, casseroles, and an assortment of vegetable recipes, such as squash (marrow) sprinkled with ginger, or pumpkin fritters, and also preserves. 'Boerekos', farmers' food, is found everywhere. Look out for *boerewors* (home-made sausage), *bredies* (stews made from lamb or mutton and vegetables), and Cape Brandy pudding.

Above: not for lightweights
Right: local tastes abound

● Many South African specialities are derived from Malaysian cuisine – a legacy from the 17th century, when Indonesian slaves imported to the Cape by the Dutch were sometimes used as cooks in white households. In and around Cape Town in particular, mildly spicy

Malay dishes have established a firm foothold on the menus of restaurants and hotels. Look out for curries, chutneys (sweet-and-sour fruit conserves served as a condiment with curries) and pickles. *Bobotie* – ground lamb spiced up with turmeric and covered with egg custard, then baked, and served with yellow rice and raisins for a sweet-tasting result – is the signature dish of this culinary style. Also very popular are pickled fish, and *sosaties* – skewered lamb or pork with small onions and usually marinated in a curry sauce. *Koeksusters* are only

for those with a pronounced sweet tooth: these delicacies are small cakes fried in fat before being immersed in syrup.

● The food that sustained the British empire is known throughout the world: eggs and bacon for breakfast, hearty roast meat lunches – beef with Yorkshire pudding and boiled vegetables – followed by sticky puddings, and Earl Grey at tea time. For white South Africans, Christmas means roast turkey, bread sauce and fruit pudding doused in brandy, all eaten in soaring temperatures, often by the pool.

● Indigenous black African cuisine – unrefined cereals, vegetables and fruit, chicken and red meat – can be found in its authentic form in rural areas. Prepared in traditional ways, it's an acquired taste, but native cooking styles are becoming more frequent in modern South African kitchens. For example, you might enjoy a dish consisting of tomato, red peppers and onions added to sorghum (a grass-like plant) and topped with French dressing.

Other contributions have been made by Bengali migrant workers – rice and Indian food mixed with Malay culinary traditions to produce something peculiarly South African, and by Portuguese settlers from Mozambique – prawns peri-peri, a seafood

dish in a marinade made from ingredients such as chillis and olive oil.

Numerous restaurants serve prawns peri-peri, as do many of those hosting a *braai* (barbecue). *Braaivleis* is as fundamentally intrinsic to the South African way of life as sunshine and rugby. There's hardly a picnic spot, campsite or bungalow in the national parks that hasn't got a barbecue and grill. A number of hotels also offer *braais* in their gardens at weekends. An important ingredient of *braaivleis* is *boerewors*, a large sausage made of mutton and beef.

Biltong delights the hearts of South Africans living abroad. Resembling dry sticks of wood, these strips of beef are salted, spiced and air-dried. A delicacy is venison biltong: when a game farmer produces his own, it leaves the commercially prepared product in the dust.

Beverages

When it comes to beverages, you should know that fruit juices and mediocre wine are sold in 3- or 5-litre containers that have a little tap on the side to ensure that the contents aren't too exposed to air and remain fresh. Liquifruit and Monis juices are produced without the addition of sugar.

The flavour of *Rooibos* tea lies somewhere

Above: Cape Tonians love to eat out
Right: the waiter went thataway

between the better-known herbal teas and black tea. It's made from the fine twigs of the local red bush and is quite refreshing when chilled. You can get it in most hotels and restaurants, and in virtually any local store.

The local mineral water, Skoonspruit (Clean Spring) is cheaper than the imported product. If there isn't any mineral water, you'll have to make do with soda.

When it comes to wine, the country's reputation as a centre of viticulture has grown in recent years. Since the end of the apartheid era, wine-makers have been at pains to learn new skills to complement the Germanic and Huguenot traditions that have served the local industry so well.

If you like liqueurs, try the mandarin-flavoured Amarula. Made from the fruit of the marula tree, it's the local equivalent of Cointreau. Also extremely sweet is the similarly flavoured Van der Hum.

The city is well served by restaurants: some good for the food, others for the buzz. Cape Tonians love to eat out, especially if they can drink their local wine. South Africans take great pride in the excellence of their own wines. Local labels fill most wine lists, leaving imports to the smaller sections at the back. Unfortunately restaurant service is not always what it should be and poor service is the bane of local diners.

In the following listing, $$$ = R220, $$ = R180, $ = up to R100, for two without wine.

Fine Dining

The Atlantic Grill
The Table Bay Hotel
Victoria & Alfred Waterfront
Tel: 021-406 5688
www.suninternational.com/resorts/tablebay/
Meals on a par with those of any world-class hotel. Summer: breakfast and dinner daily, Sunday jazz brunch. Closed in winter. $$$

Aubergine
39 Barnet Street
Gardens
Tel: 021-465 4909
www.aubergine.co.za
Set in a 19th-century townhouse, this is the place for traditional Cape favourites with a distinctly French slant. Lunch Mon–Fri, dinner Mon–Sat, and Sun in summer. $$

Au Jardin
Vineyard Hotel
Colinton Road
Newlands
Tel: 021-683 1520
www.aujardin.co.za
Classic dishes with a novel twist. Lunch Tues–Fri, dinner Mon–Sat. May–Aug closed Mon. $$$

Buitenverwachting
Klein Constantia Road
Constantia
Tel: 021-794 3522
www.buitenverwachting.co.za
Set in a Cape Dutch homestead in the middle of a wine estate. International menu with local and oriental highlights. The excellent home farm wine is recommended. Lunch Tues–Fri, dinner Tues–Sat. $$$

Constantia Uitsig
Uitsig Farm
Constantia
Tel: 021-794 4480
www.constantiauitsig.co.za
This vineyard restaurant serves what is probably the best food in the city. New World cuisine with a definite Mediterranean influence. Fish and game are specialities. Lunch Tues–Sun, dinner daily. $$$

Leinster Hall
7 Weltevreden Street
Gardens

Tel: 021-424 1836
Lovely historical manor house right in the city centre. Food is classic haute cuisine.$$$

The Restaurant
51a Somerset Road
Green Point
Tel: 021-419 2921
Quite chic, but the food, although first-class, can be pretentious. Dinner Mon–Sat. $$$

The Savoy Cabbage
Heritage Square
Cape Town
Tel: 021-424 2626
Hearty food, sometimes in odd combinations, with notable local influence. The city-centre building is an interesting blend of old and new. Lunch Mon–Fri, dinner Mon–Sat. $$

Easy Eating

All of the following are moderately priced and have good wine lists; most acknowledge in some way the traditions of local cuisine. Expect the very freshest ingredients, a choice of at least two fish dishes, and a pleasant buzz.

Beluga
The Foundry
Prestwich Street
Green Point
Tel: 021-418 2948/9

www.beluga.co.za
Good for game fish and smoked ostrich. Fine wines. Restaurant: lunch, dinner; café: breakfast, teas, lunch, dinner. Mon–Sat. $$

Cape to Cuba
Main Road
Kalk Bay
Tel: 021-788 1566
Lunch and dinner daily. Busy and buzzy with an emphasis on Cuban food. $

La Colombe
Constantia Uitsi
Constantia
Tel: 021-794 2390
www.lacolombe.co.za
First-class Provençale food with Cape flavours. Always busy. Estate wines. Lunch Mon, Wed, Sun, dinner Mon, Wed, Sat. $$

Limoncello
8 Breda Street
Gardens
Tel: 021-461 5100
Fantastic pasta and salads in tiny Italian trattoria. Lunch Mon–Fri, Dinner Mon–Sat. $

La Perla
Beach Road
Sea Point
Tel: 021-434 2471
Italian restaurant, the place for seafood. $$

Wijnhuis
Kildare Centre
Kildare Road
Newlands
Tel: 021-671 9705
Seafood, pasta, linefish and steaks, plus good local wine. Breakfast, lunch, dinner daily. $$

Willoughby & Co
Shop 6132
V & A Waterfront
Tel: 021-418 6115
Best sushi. Lunch, snacks, dinner daily. $$

Cosmopolitan

Africa Café
108 Shortmarket Street, Heritage Square
Cape Town
Tel: 021-422 3288

Above: many hotels and restaurants feature traditional European interiors
Right: a typically relaxed Camps Bay eatery

www.africacafe.co.za
Specialises in authentic combinations assembled from all over Africa. Worth trying. Lunch by arrangement, dinner Mon–Sat. $

Anatoli
24 Napier Street, Cape Town
Tel: 021-419 2501
www.anatoli.co.za
Particularly good for Turkish *meze* (a selection of hors d'oeuvre). Dinner Tues–Sun. $

Bukhara
33 Church Street,
Cape Town
Tel: 021-424 0000
www.bukhara.co.za
Excellent north Indian cuisine. Lunch Mon–Sat, dinner daily. $$

Cape Malay Restaurant
The Cellars-Hohenhort
93 Brommersvlei Road
Constantia
Tel: 021-794 2137
www.relaischateaux.com/cellars
The very best in traditional Cape Malay food. Dinner daily. Apr–Oct: closed Tues, Wed. $$

Mainland China
76 Main Road,
Claremont
Tel: 021-674 2654

Simple Chinese fare, some of the best in town. Lunch Wed–Mon. Dinner daily. $$

Mama Africa
178 Long Street
Tel: 021-424 8634
Food from Cape to Kenya and beyond. Dinner Mon–Sat. $

Milano
Main Road,
Kenilworth
Tel: 021-762 0154
Mainstream. Dinner Tues–Sun. $$

Saigon
Cape Swiss Hotel
Cnr. Kloof and Camp Streets,
Gardens
Tel: 021-424 7670/669
Authentic Vietnamese restaurant. Lunch Fri–Sun. Dinner daily. $

Vilamoura
Broadwalk Centre,
Victoria Road
Camps Bay
Tel: 021-438 1850
www.vilamoura.co.za
Cuisine influenced by the Portuguese colonists of yore. The superb seafood is especially recommended. Lunch, dinner daily. $$$

NIGHTLIFE

As befits a sophisticated, international city, Cape Town offers a diverse selection of after-hours entertainment options. Whereas you'll find any number of cinemas and theatres scattered throughout the city, you should head for the **southern suburbs** if you want to take advantage of the best choice of pubs and nightclubs congregated in a single area. If you prefer to take your entertainment in daylight hours, **Ratanga Junction**, the city's biggest amusement park, is situated just north of the city on the N1.

From the beginning of summer, open-air events become extremely popular; in winter the Victoria & Alfred Waterfront is probably the most attractive entertainment option.

By contrast, the clubs and bars *(shebeens)* in the townships and on the Cape Flats aren't exactly designed for visits by foreign tourists. These establishments, which tend to be informal, and generally patronised by labourers as after-work pit stops, are bars rather than lounges.

If you do decide to visit a *shebeen*, you should, for your own safety, go with a chaperone, especially if it is your first visit. Alternatively, some tour operators organise township trips *(see Itinerary 4, page 32)*. Whatever form of entertainment you're after, check the monthly *Cape Review* for listings.

Jazz & Live Music

Jazz is very popular in Cape Town. You can catch live performances in specialised venues, pubs, and also in supper- or small theatre-type venues.

Dizzy Jazz Café, near Camps Bay beach, is one of the oldest restaurant-jazz venues.

Light and airy, the V&A Arcade's **Green Dolphin** at the Waterfront is very popular.

Klaus's Jazz Club, at the corner of Wale and Loop streets, features big-name African artists and suitably big sounds.

Wine and dine at **Indigo**, a live jazz venue on Shortmarket and Long streets' corner.

The Natural Café (Victoria Junction Hotel in Somerset Road, Green Point) is a sophisticated live-music venue.

Mama Africa in Long Street features African music such as vibey marimba bands.

Chilli 'n Lime at the Longkloof Studios in Gardens has live music and cabaret shows.

The Barleycorn Music Club (River Club in Observatory) hosts popular folk evenings. All are invited to join jamming sessions.

A number of taverns and township *shebeens*, such as Smokies (Nyanga East), Tigers (Langa) and Duma's Falling Leaves (Gugulethu) feature music from 6.30pm to around 9pm. For further details, contact New World Music Township Tours (tel: 021-448 0203), which will take you there.

Above: a pub in the southern suburbs

Kirstenbosch Botanical Gardens hosts open-air sunset concerts of classical, jazz and big-band music during the summer months. For those with seriously eclectic tastes in music, live performances in Cape Town are reviewed in the Music Website (www.music.org.za) and listed in the 'Top of the Times' supplement of Friday's *Cape Times*, and in the weekly *Mail & Guardian*.

Nightclubs

The nightclub scene centres on **lower Long Street** and in the suburb of **Green Point**. Patrons of café society are attracted to **Kloof Street**, while students and hippies congregate in the southern suburb of **Observatory**. Just down the road from Gardens, adjacent to the city centre, **Dunkley Square** attracts an older, more sophisticated crowd. There is a gay scene in **Somerset Road** and in some parts of **Sea Point**.

On the Atlantic seaboard, **Camps Bay** is a fashionable night-time venue with a wide range of bars and restaurants.

Cape Town's club scene ranges from sophisticated live-music, dance-and-dine venues for the older crowd to warehouse-type venues with a number of rooms, several DJs, playstations, lasers and special lighting effects. Disco-style party or rave clubs cater for the younger crowd. For a detailed account of the club scene, consult Evan Milton's 'Bandstand' column in the 'Tonight' section of Tuesday's and Thursday's *Cape Argus*.

Dockside
Century City, Ratanga Junction, Milnerton
Tel: 021-552 2030
Dockside is one of South Africa's biggest nightclubs, with 14 bars, three restaurants and four storeys. Saturday's all-night entertainment packs in around 6,000 revellers.

The Fez
Hout Street, Cape Town
Tel: 021-423 1456
Sip evening cocktails in plush surroundings to house music played by popular DJs.

The Jet Lounge
74 Long Street, Cape Town
Tel: 021-426 1506

Trendy, upbeat party venue for funk, house and Latino music.

Kapitol
Pepper Street, Cape Town
Mainstream, over-21s venue known for attracting Cape Town's models.

Plum Crazi
Long Street, Cape Town
Three floors and a roof garden. Attracts mainstream over-21 crowd.

Southern suburbs:
Fubar
80 Main Road, Claremont
Tel: 021-671 5535
A spacious venue that mainly attracts mature singles.

Springfields II
Next to the railway station, Newlandst
Predominantly a DJ venue.

Taboo
Main Road, Claremont
Predominantly a DJ venue.

Three Arts Theatre
Main Road, Plumstead
Tel: 021-761 2949
The place for teenage parties. Over-19s are barred, as is alcohol.

Pubs and Bars
The Boer and Brit
Alphen Hotel
Constantia
Sedate, nostalgic atmosphere. Can be a refreshing alternative to the noise and bustle of most bars.

Right: play pool at Rolling Stone

The Bronx
Corner of Strand, Napier streets, Cape Town
Small bar and gay cabaret venue.

Buddha Bar
Somerset Road,
Green Point
Upmarket lounge bar for trendy set.

Café Manhattan
Waterkant Street
Laid-back gay venue.

Dunes
Hout Bay
Another choice venue for an evening drink.

La Med
Clifton
Excellent place for sundowners after a day
on the beach.

Perseverance Tavern
Buitenkant Street
Affectionately known to regulars as 'The
Percy', this is the country's oldest registered
tavern and probably the closest you'll get
to an English-style pub in the City Bowl.

Purple Turtle
Corner of Shortmarket, Long streets
Trendy bar incorporating an internet café.

The Red Herring
Noordhoek
Another agreeable venue for sundowners
after a day on the beach.

Rhodes House
60 Queen Victoria Street, Gardens
Up-market cocktail bar situated in a super-
plush building. Attracts a fashionable crowd.

Rolling Stone
Observatory
A place for pool players.

The V&A Waterfront
This entertainment neighbourhood has a
wide variety of great drinking holes. Sports
fans should note that these include a number
of sports bars with large-screen televisions.

Cafés

Café Bardeli
Kloof Street
An excellent place for a nocturnal espresso.

Café Carte Blanche
Trill Road, Observatory
Long-standing establishment that's excellent
for coffee, cake and flamboyant people.

Café Camissa
Kloof Street
Just down the road from Café Paradiso, this
is another spot for coffee-drinking night birds.

Café Paradiso
Kloof Street
Mature, European-style café comparable to
the late-opening Bardeli and a good choice.

Long Street Café
Central Cape Town
Manhattan-type café.

Obz Café
115 Lower Main Road
Observatory
Popular establishment similar in character to
the laid-back late-night cafés on Kloof Street.

Above: anything goes where pub society's dress code is concerned
Right: the Victoria & Alfred Waterfront is a splendid sight at night

Cinemas

Labia Theatre
Orange Street, Gardens
Tel: 424 5927
www.labia.co.za
This is the oldest independent art-repertory cinema in the country in what was originally an Italian embassy ballroom. Old-world ambience and a cosy bar for hot chocolate.

IMAX theatre
BMW Pavilion, V&A Waterfront
Large-screen cinematics.

Benson & Hedges open-air cinema
Glen Cove, Camps Bay
Annual event.

Ster Kinekor and Nu Metro cinemas
These two chains have cinemas in most of the city's large shopping centres. You can buy tickets for movies (as well as shows and concerts) through Computicket, an electronic booking agency that operates in most of these centres (tel: 011-340 8000 or 083-915-8000; www.computicket.co.za).

Theatres

Artscape
Foreshore
Tel: 021-421 7839
www.artscape.co.za
Ballet, opera and mainly mainstream drama.

Baxter Theatre Centre
Main Road, Rondebosch
Tel: 021-685 7880
www.baxter.co.za
Ballet, opera and mainstream productions.

Theatre on the Bay
Camps Bay
Tel: 021-438 3301/33
www.theatreonthebay.co.za
Cocktails and snacks before the show.

The Little Theatre
Orange Street, Gardens
Tel: 021-480 7129
Fringe productions.

On Broadway
Somerset Road, Green Point
Tel: 021-418 8338
www.onbroadway.co.za
Fringe productions.

Maynardville Open-Air Theatre
Wynberg
Tel: 021-421 7695
Regular Shakespearean productions. Bring a picnic and enjoy drama under the stars.

The Armchair Theatre
Lower Main Road, Observatory
Tel: 021-447 1514
Stand-up comedy and other live gigs.

CALENDAR OF EVENTS

The Christmas season is the busiest time of the year. Offices close for up to three weeks and ever-increasing numbers of holiday-makers flock into town to enjoy the seaside. Even at weekends – which, in effect, begin after lunch on Fridays when office workers knock off early – the roads into and out of town are clogged. So much for the sleepy city, or 'slaapstad' as Cape Town is known. You should therefore be aware of the many diverse holidays, festivals and public events that occur in the city throughout the year.

January

1 January: *New Year's Day*. It seems that everyone in the city has piled onto the beach. Holiday atmosphere pervades everything. *Coon Carnival*. A street carnival with singing, dancing and bright costumes. January–February: *Maynardville Open-air Theatre*. Shakespeare plays performed alfresco. Take a picnic.

February

North Sea Jazz Festival. Africa's largest jazz festival.

March

21 March: *Human Rights Day* marks some of the darkest days of the country's recent past, when human rights were denied to the majority of the population. *Argus Cycle Tour*. The 105-km (66-mile) annual race is the culmination of the International Cycling Competition.

April

21 April: *Family Day* combines the joys of Mother's Day and Father's Day. *Two Oceans Marathon*. A 56-km (35-mile) route attracts over 8,000 runners. 27 April: *Freedom Day* commemorates the first occasion on which South Africans of all races were allowed to vote. *Decorex*. Every second year, this up-market event exhibits work by interior designers and the latest in home accessories. April–May: *Cape Town International Film Festival*. A mixed bag of local features and big-name international movies screened at different venues.

May

1 May: *Workers Day*. A holiday in honour of workers that's comparable to May Day celebrations elsewhere in the world May–June: *Design for Living Exhibition*. A lifestyle show featuring furniture, decor accessories, clothes and appliances.

June

16 June: *Youth Day* commemorates the tragic 1976 Soweto riots, in which young people figured heavily.

July

14 July: *Bastille Day*. The anniversary of the storming of the Bastille in 1789 is still widely celebrated in places where there are communities descended from French Huguenots, such as Franschhoek.

August

9 August: *National Women's Day*

September

24 September: *Heritage Day*
25 September: public holiday
Wild-Flower Show at Darling. Well-timed to coincide with the appearance of millions of wild-flowers along the arid west coast. September–November : *Whale-watching*. The Southern Right Whale comes to the Cape coast to spawn. Once nearly extinct, this is now a thriving species.

November

Nedbank Summer Concert Season. Musical performances from jazz to classical.

December

Mother City Queer Project. Increasingly, gays from all over the world come to Cape Town for the local version of Mardi Gras, a huge themed (costume dress) party. *Kirstenbosch Summer Sunset Concerts*. Excellent musical performances in the famous botanical gardens. Take a picnic. 16 December: *Day of Reconciliation* 25 December : *Christmas Day* 26 December : *Day of Goodwill* December–March : *Spier Summer Festival*. A first-class, summer arts festival held near Stellenbosch at an historic Cape Dutch farm.

Right: Cape Town enjoys holidays, festivals and public celebrations throughout the year

Practical Information

GETTING THERE

By Air

As a visitor to South Africa you might expect to touch down at Johannesburg International Airport, but there is an increasing number of direct scheduled flights to Cape Town International Airport from a variety of European airports. It's good to know that if you have to arrive via Johannesburg, Cape Town is only two hours away by air, so the onward flight shouldn't present any difficulties. There are plenty of good deals for charter flights to both cities from Europe, so shop around. Tickets in the high season, during the Christmas period, can be much more expensive than at other times of the year.

By Rail

It is possible to travel to Cape Town from Johannesburg or Pretoria by train. Given the length of the journey (about 24 hours from Pretoria), you will probably want to do it in comfort, if not in style, which means that you should travel on the Blue Train. This is expensive but it does have luxurious accommodation, a dining car and a lounge car. The price of sleeping arrangements vary from expensive to moderate.

The best reason for taking the train can be seen through the window – the views of the landscape are wonderful. For reservations, tel: 021-449 2672. Another option is Rovos Rail, a private train service for tourists. If you want to explore beyond Cape Town, you can take a Rovos train to many other places – it's the last word in luxury. For details, tel: 012-421 4020 (Pretoria).

There are regular intercity trains which, though efficient, don't match the standards of their European or American counterparts. The comprehensive national rail network has three classes of travel. For information, and reservations (which are essential), tel: 086-000 8888. Book first- and second-class tickets at least 24 hours in advance.

Left: Greenmarket Square market
Right: a bargain on Long Street

By Bus

Road travel is a great way to see the land – it's quite possible to travel to Cape Town by bus. Coaches cover most of the country, including towns and villages in the interior that you would otherwise be unlikely to see. The service is inexpensive and you can hop on or off as you like. This means of travel may not be luxurious but it is comfortable.

Greyhound: tel: 083 915 9000
Translux: tel: 021-449 3333
Intercape: tel: 021-380 4400

By Road

Three major highways, the N1, the N2 and the N7, link Cape Town with the rest of the country. From Johannesburg take the N1, a mostly single-lane artery that traverses almost the entire country. Be warned that local drivers tend to be unpredictable, which makes this busy route somewhat dangerous. So be extra vigilant, particularly at night when the traffic is surprisingly heavy. The countryside en route is quite diverse – by the time you arrive in Cape Town some 1,400km (875 miles) later, you'll have a very good idea of the lie of the land. Some travellers opt for an overnight break at, say, Victoria West.

The N1 enters Cape Town directly, on the portside foreshore area, at the bottom of Buitengracht Street, where there are signs to various parts of the city. Follow signs to Sea Point for the Atlantic seaboard (Bantry Bay, Clifton and Camps Bay). For the Southern Suburbs, head for Eastern Boulevard, which

climbs a flank of Devil's Peak, heads around the mountain and approaches Newlands and Claremont via Paradise Road.

For Llandudno and Hout Bay, continue up Buitengracht Street and over Kloof Nek, staying on Camps Bay Drive till the intersection with Victoria Road. Turn left here and continue on the coast to Llandudno.

Take the N2 coastal road if you're heading for Plettenberg Bay via the Garden Route. The N7 is the west-coast highway that leads to Namibia.

TRAVEL ESSENTIALS

Visas and Passports

A valid passport entitles European nationals to stay in South Africa for up to six months, visitors from the United States, Canada, New Zealand and Australia up to three months. You must also have either a return ticket, or proof that you are in a position to buy one. On entering the country, you will be required to fill in a temporary-residence permit stating the reason for, and duration of, your visit.

When to Visit

The best time to visit Cape Town is when all the tourists have left, ie, after Christmas. The weather generally remains very hot until the end of February. Then, until the end of April, the days are still sunny and pleasantly warm. At this time of year you shouldn't have a problem booking a restaurant table, finding parking (the roads are far less crowded), or grabbing a quiet, secluded sunbathing spot on the beach. It's generally cool until about mid-December, after which the heat is on. If you can't stand the heat, come in the dead of winter (July and August) when it rains. It never gets really cold unless a rare arctic breeze blows into the city from the snow-capped country mountains.

If you're attracted by razzmatazz, crowded beaches and hectic nightlife, then come for Christmas and New Year's Eve. Cape Town is becoming more and more busy over the festive season as the world wakes up to its myriad attractions.

Clothing

Cape Town is known for its informality. Businessmen rarely go to work in a suit and, when they do, they are unlikely to bother with a tie. Chinos and T-shirts are quite acceptable for restaurant dinners; jackets are surplus to requirements at even the finest restaurants. In summer it's too hot to wear anything but shorts or short skirts. So bring the minimum, but pack a sweater or shawl in case there are sudden temperature changes

Above: parasols protect shoppers from a hot sun in Greenmarket Square

or you plan to travel to the mountains for the weekend. Beach-oriented summer days can be spent in a sarong (for both men and women). Or you could follow the example of Nelson Mandela and wear a Madiba shirt, which you will be able to pick up cheaply at the market in Greenmarket Square in the centre of town.

You should also bring a hat or baseball cap for protection from the sun, which is strong and potentially dangerous. Sandals, flip-flops and sneakers are the most popular everyday footwear. If you prefer to be more formal, choose loafers. If you're label-conscious, bring your JP Tod's and the like with you from home because, although it is possible to buy most things in Cape Town, designer shops are fairly few and far between, and also expensive.

GETTING ACQUAINTED

Geography

The city's narrow, constricted central zones are squeezed in between the sea and the mountain. The city Bowl area sits in the lap of Table Mountain, Devil's Peak and Signal Hill. Locked between the Bowl and the sea, the city centre faces Table Bay at the Victoria & Alfred waterfront. Not that long ago, the waterfront was a near-defunct industrial area; today, courtesy of a world-class rejuvenation programme, it has turned into a classy development for shopping and entertainment. The adjoining port services fishing boats and passenger liners.

The Atlantic seaboard, which houses the suburbs to the west of the city, snakes around the flank of Signal Hill, the extension of Lion's Head, taking in Sea Point, Bantry Bay, Clifton and Camps Bay.

The connecting artery is Victoria Road, which continues on to Llandudno, Hout Bay and further, to Chapman's Peak. In the northern suburbs area are Bellville and Durbanville. In the opposite direction, if you continue around the flank of Devil's Peak and follow the mountain chain to the south of the peninsula, are the southern suburbs, including Claremont, Newlands and Constantia.

Beyond the southern suburbs, about a 40-minute drive away, is False Bay. Here the coastline's picturesque seaside villages stretch in one direction to the peninsula's tip, enclosed by the Cape of Good Hope Nature Reserve, and in the other to Gordon's Bay and the coastal drive to the wonderful whale-watching territory of Hermanus.

Contrary to popular belief, the Cape Peninsula is not the tip of Africa, where the Atlantic and Indian oceans meet. That particular landmark is at Cape Agulhas, which lies a few hundred kilometres – three or four hours' drive – along the east coast (head for Bredasdorp via the N2, and then Arniston). Cape Flats, a part-desert area now home to the airport and a number of townships, is located between the city and the Hottentots Holland Mountains, over which the morning sun ascends. Somerset West lies between the Flats and the mountains.

Religion

The once-dominant role of religion in South African public life has decreased since the

Afrikaaners' Dutch Reformed Church lost the ascendancy. There are, however, a large number of Christian churches of various denominations, and also synagogues, mosques (Islam has quite a strong presence in the Cape) and Hindu temples (though these are more common in Durban than in Cape Town). The independent African Churches mix traditional tribal beliefs with Western influences.

Above: one of several synagogues that serve the city's Jewish community

MONEY MATTERS

The unit of local currency is the rand, which is divided into 100 cents. Bring travellers' cheques and a small amount of local currency. Hotels do change money, but they charge a fee, so a trip to a bank is probably your best bet. Banking hours are 9am–3.30pm on weekdays, and 9–11am on Saturdays, and most major branches have foreign-exchange facilities. Alternatively you'll find a 24-hour foreign-exchange service at the Victoria & Alfred Waterfront.

Most major credit cards are accepted in the majority of restaurants and shops, and there are any number of ATM machines in the city centre (especially in shopping malls and streets, banks, and even at petrol stations). If you want to carry a large amount of cash (which is not advisable), check the set daily limit for withdrawals. Remember to bring your PIN number with you if you intend to draw funds from ATMs.

Bear in mind that you will need cash for incidentals such as taxi rides and petrol (for which you cannot pay by credit card), in bars and for tips and so on.

In a country that has become notorious for its astronomical crime levels, you should observe the following basic guidelines. Never carry large amounts of cash – rather cash cheques every other day or as frequently as you need to. Be inconspicuous with your cash in the streets – keep your wallet or purse hidden. Don't withdraw money from an ATM machine in a deserted area.

GETTING AROUND

Airport Connections
The airport is about 20km (12 miles) from town, to which the taxi fare should be about R120. Taxis are plentiful outside both domestic and international arrivals halls. Bus transfers are far cheaper, although a little slower (around 40 minutes). For a door-to-door airport shuttle service, try:
    Legend Tours: tel: 021-697 4056
    Magic Bus: tel: 021-505 6300

Buses, Taxis
The urban bus service is slow, sporadic, erratic and in need of modernisation. As for taxis, there are two distinct services, of which the minibus option should be avoided. Minibus drivers tend to pack passengers in like sardines before setting off at breakneck pace with little regard for anyone's safety. If you must use a minibus – you can stand on almost any main artery and flag one down – only do so during daylight hours.

Rather use metered taxis which, although more expensive, are safer and more reliable. The drivers even know where they're going. But you can't hail one on the street and, because you have to call ahead for your ride, the meter starts ticking before your journey has even started. Look in the Yellow Pages for numbers. Marine Taxis (tel: 021-434 0434), which serves the city centre area, is a well-known, reliable company.

Trains
The railway terminus is a busy, thronging locale, but to most tourists it's useful only for catching the suburban train that goes to the False Bay coast, stopping at Simonstown, or as a departure point for upcountry trains. The coastal trip is lovely from Muizenberg, after which the train stops at all the coastal 'villages' by the sea. If you don't have a car and want to swim, take this train to any of the stops from, and including, Muizenberg.

All the stations are near beaches. Remember to check the times of returning trains before leaving the station, and don't travel back after dusk. For your own security, you should travel in the first-class section and, if possible, with company. Cape Metro Rail, tel: 021-449 6478.

Left: a car-rental firm sets out its stall

Driving

If you're staying in a hotel in a suburb near the city centre, and if you're not averse to walking, then it's easy to get about in a taxi. But for greater convenience you will need a car. (You shouldn't rely on public transport.) The roads are generally excellent and destinations are mostly well-signposted. Parking facilities are, however, limited; if you park in an unauthorised place, you should expect to be fined or clamped. Don't be surprised to find an unofficial parking attendant offering his facilities. As a rule of thumb, it's okay to use these in exchange for a small tip, if only to prevent your rear windows being smashed by street kids. Never leave anything remotely valuable in a visible position in the car. Rather lock it in the trunk. To hire a car, try one of the following international companies:

Avis: tel: 021-934 0330
Budget: tel: 086 101 6622
Hertz: tel: 021-386 1560
Imperial: tel: 021-448 5608

Consult the Yellow Pages or the tourist information office for a long list of smaller local rental companies, many of which offer excellent deals. These firms do make a per-kilometre charge over and above a rental fee, but you might be able to strike a deal that allows you a set amount of kilometres free each day, over which you pay the per-kilometre rate. To rent a car you must be over the age of 23 and in possession of a valid driver's licence.

OPENING TIMES

Shops and businesses tend to open early in Cape Town – it's not uncommon for local white-collar workers to be summoned to an 8am meeting. Most shops are open 8.30am–5pm on weekdays, and 9am–1am on Saturdays. Most stores on the Victoria and Alfred Waterfront are open until 9pm, seven days a week. Sunday is – V&A Waterfront stores notwithstanding – still a day of rest.

ACCOMMODATION

The following is a listing of hotels and guesthouses, with prices graded according to the chart below. The city and its suburbs are well served by first-class guesthouses, which often make for more congenial stopovers than hotels.

$$$$ – R1500–2500 for a double
$$$ – R800–R1500 for a double
$$ – R500–R800 for a double
$ – up to R500 for two

Above: Darling's Evita se Perron station

City Centre
Hotels
Cape Grace Hotel
West Quay, V&A Waterfront
Cape Town 8001
Tel: 021-410 7100
Fax: 021-419 7622
www.capegrace.com
One of the country's most luxurious and elegant hotels, the Cape Grace is in the heart of town, right on the harbour. It has wonderful views, a magnificently situated swimming pool and a first-class restaurant. $$$$

Cape Heritage Hotel
Heritage Square, 92 Bree Street
Cape Town 8001.
Tel: 021-424 4646
Fax: 021-424 4949
www.capestay.co.za/capeheritage
Situated in what is probably Cape Town's oldest surviving section in Heritage Square, this establishment features rooms reflecting the city's multicultural heritage. $$

Capetonian Protea Hotel
Pier Place, Heerengracht, PO Box 6856
Roggebaai, Cape Town 8012
Tel: 021-692 1260
Fax: 021-691 7079
Friendly establishment right on the Waterfront. Air-conditioning, telephone in rooms, non-smoking rooms available and pool. $$$

The Cullinan
Lower Buitengracht Street, Cape Town 8001
Tel: 021-418 6920
Fax: 021-418 3559

A huge, somewhat impersonal establishment on the foreshore, this is Cape Town's newest addition to an already burgeoning list of places to stay. A stone's throw from both waterfront and city centre, it's ideal for shoppers. $$$

Holiday Inn Capetown
Strand Street, PO Box 4532
Cape Town 8000
Tel: 021-488 5100
Fax: 021-423 8875
www.ichotelsgroup.com
Part of the international chain, the Cape Sun is a luxury hotel in the centre of Cape Town. It has air-conditioning, telephone in rooms, non-smoking rooms available, facilities for disabled guests, restaurant, fitness centre and pool. Prices depend on availability. Special deals sometimes operate. $$$

Holiday Inn Waterfront
1 Lower Buitengracht Street
Cape Town 8001
Tel: 021-409 4000
Fax: 021-409 4444
www.ichotelsgroup.com
Not to be confused with its foreign namesake. This is a member of a local chain, owned by Southern Sun. It provides good-value family-oriented accommodation at an affordable price. $$$

The Table Bay
Quay 6, V&A Waterfront, Cape Town 8001
Tel: 021-406 5000
Fax: 021-406 5656
www.suninternational.com/resorts/tablebay/
This glamorous hotel has lavish, international-style accommodation. Like the Cape Grace, it's on the harbour and has magnificent views of sea and mountain. $$$$

Victoria & Alfred Hotel
Pierhead, V&A Waterfront, Cape Town 8001
Tel: 021-419 6677
Fax: 021-419 8955
www.vahotel.co.za
Well-situated for shopping in the Waterfront mall, this hotel, with its attractive, colonial-style rooms, has magnificent views of the harbour and Table Mountain. Be sure to have a meal at the excellent restaurant. $$$–$$$$

Above: the lavish Table Bay hotel has magnificent views of Table Mountain and the harbour

City Bowl
Hotel
The Mount Nelson
76 Orange Street, Gardens
Cape Town 8001
Tel: 021-483 1000
Fax: 021-483 1782
www.mountnelson.co.za
The pale pink 'Nellie' is an old-style grand hotel that has become an international landmark for discerning travellers since opening in 1899. It has two swimming pools and, even if you're not staying here, you should sample its afternoon teas. Close to the city centre, it's within easy walking distance of the shops and museums. $$$$

Guesthouses
Acorn House
1 Montrose Avenue
Oranjezicht
Cape Town 8001
Tel: 021-461 1782
Fax: 021-461 1768
www.acornhouse.co.za
With spectacular mountain, harbour and city views, this colonial-style guesthouse built in 1904 is a charming place to stay with a lovely garden, $

Cape Corner
25 Burnside Road, Tamboerskloof
Cape Town 8001
Tel/fax: 021-422 1363
www.capecorner.co.za
Lovely Victorian terraced house near busy Kloof Street's shops and restaurants. $$

De Waterkant Lodge and Cottages
20 Loader Street, De Waterkant
Cape Town 8001
Tel: 021-419 1097
Fax: 021-419 1077
www.dewaterkant.co.za
Set in a quaint neighbourhood and with fine views over the harbour to Robben Island. Also 10 self-catering cottages. $$$

Ikhaya Guest Lodge
Dunkley Square and Wandel Street,
Gardens, Cape Town 8001
Tel: 021-461 8880
Fax: 021-461 8889

www.ikhayalodge.co.za
Ikhaya (meaning 'home' in Xhosa), an unusual take on the 'bush' in an urban setting, is a regular favouirte for visiting models and film crews. It is conveniently situated for the city centre. No swimming pool. $$

Inn with a View
127a Kloofnek Road, Tamboerskloof
Cape Town 8001
Tel: 021-424 5220
Fax: 021-424 5293
www.innwithaview.co.za
Gets its name from the magnificent views of Table Mountain, which towers over the hotel. Comfortable rooms. $$

Kensington Place
38 Kensington Crescent, Higgovale,
Cape Town 8001
Tel: 021-424 4744
Fax: 021-424 1810
www.kensingtonplace.co.za
Perhaps the best guesthouse or small hotel in the city. Kensington Place is chic, and, in a city not known for its attention to customers' needs, it offers excellent quality of service. It also has a swimming pool and a pretty garden. $$$$

Lady Victoria Guesthouse
1 Kelvin Street, Upper Gardens
Cape Town 8001
www.ladyvictoria.co.za
Tel/fax: 021-423 3814
This guesthouse is an authentic Victorian mansion situated on the lower slopes of Table Mountain. It is within easy walking distance of the city centre. $

Right: the grand Mount Nelson hotel has become an international landmark

Rosedene
28 Upper Kloof Street, Higgovale
Cape Town 8001
Tel: 021-424 3290
Fax: 021-424 3481
www.rosedene.co.za
At the foot of Table Mountain, Rosedene has gorgeous views, and eclectic variety of furniture. $$

The Walden House
5 Burnside Road, Tamboerskloof
Cape Town 8001
Tel: 021-424 4256
Fax: 021-424 0547
www.walden-house.com
A magnificent Victorian homestead, the Walden House is close to Kloof Street and is convenient for shops, delis and bars. $$

Welgelegen Guest House
6 Stephen Street, Gardens, Cape Town 8001
Tel: 021-426 2373/4
Fax: 021-426 2375
www.welgelegen.co.za
A bright Victorian mansion, the Welgelegen Guest House is a place in which to relax. There's a pool at the rear, and it's close to the delis and bars of Kloof Street. The owner is happy to give rides to, say, the cable-car station at the foot of Table Mountain. $$

Atlantic Seaboard
Hotels
The Bay Hotel
69 Victoria Road, Camps Bay
Cape Town 8001
Tel: 021-430 4444
Fax: 021-438 4433
www.thebay.co.za
Virtually on Camps Bay beach, this is the only place to stay if you want a bed within two minutes' walk of the sea. $$$$

Le Vendome
20 London Road, Sea Point, Cape Town 8050
Tel: 021-430 1200
Fax: 021-430 1500
www.le-vendome.co.za
A luxurious hotel with an excellent swimming pool, Le Vendome is well placed for easy access to beaches, shops and transport facilities. $$$$

Winchester Mansions Hotel
221 Beach Road, Sea Point, Cape Town 8005
Tel: 021-434 2351
Fax: 021-434 0215
www.winchester.co.za
An old-fashioned hotel not far from the sea, Winchester Mansions has a lovely courtyard setting for cool lunches and dinners on hot summer days. Unfortunately close to the noisy Beach Road. $$

Guesthouses
The Cape Victoria
Corner of Wigtown and Torbay roads,
Green Point, Cape Town 8001
Tel/fax: 021-439 7721
www.capevictoria.co.za
Charming, friendly management, great breakfasts, lovely pool and wonderful views over Table Bay to the west Coast. All the bedrooms are very well appointed. $$

Primi Sea Castle
15 Victoria Road, Camps Bay
Cape Town 8005
Tel: 021-438 4010
Fax: 021-438 4015
Right on the beach, this is the place for luxurious, fully serviced self-catering holiday apartments. There's a pool, excellent breakfasts and views of Camps Bay and Table Mountain. $$$

Northern Suburbs
Guesthouses
Jabulani Guest House
Hafele and Windmill streets, Durbanville 7551
Tel: 021-975 2121
Fax: 021-976 3593
www.jabulaniguests.co.za
The Jabulani has a swimming pool and six suites. Particularly good for wine enthusiasts due to what is probably its best asset – a location near the little-known Durbanville Wine Route. $

The Sanctuary Guesthouse
1 Sanctuary Close, Milnerton 7441
Tel/fax: 021-552 5441
www.geocities.com/sanctuarysa/
Attractive thatched house with pool in an excellent location, with stunning views. Close to Milnerton golf course. $$

dens, and the two restaurants and wine cellar are excellent. $$$$

Constantia Uitsig Country Hotel
Constantia Uitsig Wine Estate,
Spaanschemat River Road,
Constantia 7848
Tel: 021-794 6500
Fax: 021-794 7605
www.constantiauitsig.co.za
Set in beautiful rolling vineyards, the Constantia Uitsig has 16 garden suites. Both of its restaurants are in the city's top five. A good place to choose for quiet luxury. $$$

Steenberg Country Hotel
Tokai and Steenberg Road,
Constantia 7848
Tel: 021-713 2222
Fax: 021-713 2251
www.steenberghotel.com
The Steenberg is a small hotel with an excellent restaurant, set on a historic estate at the top of Constantia amongst the oaks. Includes a world-class golf course. $$$$

The Vineyard
Colinton Road, Newlands, 7700
Tel: 021-657 4500
Fax: 021-657 4501
www.vineyard.co.za
Set in picturesque gardens, and offering fine views of the mountains, this 18th-century homestead has excellent facilities, including a heated swimming pool and well-equipped gym. The Vineyard's first-class restaurant specialises in French cuisine. $$$

Guesthouses
Canterbury House
16 Canterbury Drive, Bishopscourt 7806
Tel: 021-797 8228
Fax: 021-762 0940
www.canterburyhouse.co.za
Located in an up-market suburb, Canterbury House is a comfortable option. Its attractions include a swimming pool and floodlit tennis court. $$

Claire Cottage
18 Phyllis Road, Claremont 7708
Tel/fax: 021-797 5894
Claire Cottage, a self-catering flatlet, enjoys

Sunset Beach Villas
7 Winkle Way, Sunset Beach, 7441
Tel: 021-551 0111
Fax: 021-551 0970
www.sunset.co.za
A fine setting right on the ocean, a wonderful sun deck, a salt-water pool and great views of Table Mountain from the northern side of Table Bay all combine to make Sunset Beach Villas a recommended destination. It's also well placed for the beach and shops. $$

Southern Suburbs
Hotels
Alphen
Alphen Drive, Constantia 7848
Tel: 021-794 5011
Fax: 021-794 5710
www.alphen.co.za
A lovely 18th-century mansion situated in the mountains, the Alphen belongs to descendants of the original owners. $$$

Cellars-Hohenort
93 Brommersvlei Road, Constantia 7848
Tel: 021-794 2137
Fax: 021-794 2149
www.cellars-hohenort.com
This huge, graceful hotel was converted from 17th-century wine cellars. Among its many features are a luxurious presidential suite, good swimming pool, tennis and walking trails. It is set in beautifully landscaped gar-

Above: an option in Simonstown

an excellent location in the heart of Claremont, not far from Cavendish Square – Cape Town's leading shopping centre. Use of swimming pool. $$

Constantia Palms
3 Constantiaberg Close, Constantia 7806
Tel: 021-794 1269
Fax: 021-794 3910
www.constantiapalms.co.za
Constantia Palms' attractions include lush gardens, stunning views, vineyards and local wine. $$

Constantia Stables
8 Chantecler Lane
Constantia 7806
Tel/fax: 021-794 3653
These traditional Cape stables, converted into charming accommodation are set in the heart of vineyard-filled Constantia. $

Klein Boscheuwel Guest House
51a Klaassens Road, Constantia 7806
Tel/fax: 021-762 2323
www.kleinbosheuwel.co.za
Lovely views from most rooms; located near the vineyards. $

Wild Olive Guest House
4 Keurboom Road, Newlands 7708
Tel: 021-683 0880
Fax: 021-671 5776
www.wildolive.co.za
Conveniently situated near Cavendish Square and the cricket ground. $$

Hout Bay
Guesthouses
Frogg's Leap
Baviaans Close, Hout Bay 7706
Tel/fax: 021-790 2590
www.froggsleap.co.za
A 40-minute drive from the city centre, Frogg's Leap is a lovely plantation-style house complete with colonial-style furniture, and is located in a peaceful wooded valley. $

Lichtenstein Guest Lodge
Harbour Road, Hout Bay 7872
Tel: 021-790 2213
Fax: 021-790 2593
www.lichtensteincastle.co.za
If you're an admirer of kitsch, Lichtenstein Guest Lodge is definitely the place for you. Located high above Hout Bay, this pseudogothic castle has 12 individually decorated suites. $

Noordhoek
Guesthouses
Three Sisters Guest House
2 Yatagan Lane
Noordhoek 7985
Tel: 021-785 5357
Fax: 021-785 4181
www.threesisters.co.za
Stunning views out over Noordhoek's famous beach to the Atlantic Ocean. Two delightful rooms with tiled floors, comfortable furnishings and private terraces. Also offers a self-catering cottage. Pool. $$$$

False Bay Coast
Guesthouses
Boulders Beach
4 Boulders Place, Boulders Beach,
Simonstown 7995
Tel: 021-786 1758
Fax: 021-786 1825
www.bouldersbeach.co.za
On the way to the Cape of Good Hope Nature Reserve, this is a good option for exploring rare natural attractions such as the colony of jackass penguins at Boulders Beach and, during the whaling season, Southern Right Whales in False Bay. $

Whale Bay
402 Main Road, Murdoch Valley,
Simonstown 7975
Tel: 021-786 3291
Fax: 021-786 5453
www.whaleviewmanor.co.za
Comfortable guesthouse in fine natural environment with coastal and rural views. A short walk from the beach and a whale-watching platform. $$–$$$

Franschhoek
La Couronne
Robertsvlei Road , Franschhoek 7690
Tel: 021-876 2770
Fax: 021-876 3788
www.lacouronnehotel.co.za
Features several suites with magnificent views and a stylish in-house restaurant. $$$

La Petite Maison
La Petite Ferme,
Franschhoek Pass, Franschhoek 7690
Tel: 021-876 3016
Fax: 021-876 3624
E-mail: lapetite@iafrica.com
Good value. $$

Le Quartier Francais
16 Huguenot Road, Franschhoek 7690
Tel: 021-876 2151
Fax: 021-876 3105
www.lqf.co.za
An exceptional country-house guesthouse just outside the city, well-placed for tours of the winelands. Le Quartier Francais is small but is built round a pleasant garden courtyard with a pool. Features an acclaimed restaurant. $$$

HEALTH & EMERGENCIES

AIDS
HIV infection and Aids have become huge problems in South Africa and the instances of infection are growing rapidly. Take all the usual precautions. Condoms are freely available.

Sunburn
Skin cancer is very common among the country's white population. Always protect yourself against the sun, not just on the beach but when out walking and sightseeing. The most intense sunlight hours are from about 11am until about 3pm. On the beach always wear a hat.

Pharmacies
The laten-night Glengariff pharmacy (on the corner of Glengariff and Main roads, Sea Point, 8001; tel: 021-434 8622) is open 8.30am–11pm daily.

Useful Telephone Numbers
Police: 10111
Traffic police: 021-406 8700
Ambulance: 10177
International Directory Enquiries: 0903
National Directory Enquiries: 1023
Fire/Rescue: 021-535 1100
Operator: 1023

Crime
The country suffers a very high level of crime, and visitors can be particularly vulnerable. The following obvious steps will minimise the risk of your joining the crime statistics.
• Don't carry valuables in the open. Leave them at your hotel when going to the beach.
• Lock doors and windows when alone in your hotel or lodging, and when you go out.
• Be vigilant, especially in the city centre. Muggings occur in broad daylight, even in the busiest areas.
• Don't wander through the city centre at night, wearing expensive jewellery or talking on your mobile phone.
• Lock your car when it's parked and never leave anything on view inside it.
• Lock car doors when driving.
• Never pick up hitch-hikers.

Left: a phone call away

COMMUNICATIONS & MEDIA

Telephone

It's comparatively cheap to use the telephone in South Africa. Coin- and card-operated Telkom phones are common in the city, especially in shopping malls, post offices and the railway station. You can buy phone cards, in denominations of R15, R20, R50, R100 and R200, from newsagents and post offices.

For calls abroad, dial 09 followed by the relevant country code, as listed below, and your number.

Australia: 61
France: 33
Germany: 49
Japan: 81
Netherlands: 31
Spain: 34
UK: 44
US and Canada: 1

South Africa's national telecommunications system is very advanced, and cellular phones utilising comprehensive networks are increasingly popular. These can be hired for the duration of your stay from an outlet in the airport, car rental agencies or Cellhire at the V&A Waterfront (tel: 021-418 1313; www.hire4lower.co.uk) at rates that start at about R11 per day.

Postal Service

The main post office (weekdays 8am–4.30pm, Sat 8am–noon) is located at Grand Central Building, on the corner of Plein and Darling streets, Cape Town 8001 (tel: 021-464 1700). You can also buy stamps at some book shops, supermarkets and a host of other outlets.

The national postal service is not very reliable. It's extremely slow and there is no guarantee that your letter or parcel will ever reach its destination. However, mail can be registered, sent by express or by Fastmail and Speed Services. This way you have a record of what's been sent.

Foreign Newspapers

Foreign newspapers and magazines are widely available but tend to be dated by the time they arrive. Expect the London *Times* to be up to a week old. Exclusive Books on the Victoria & Alfred Waterfront is the best source for *The Times* and *The Herald Tribune*. Also try the CNA newsagent chain – its Waterfront branch has a good selection that includes the *The Daily Telegraph*, *The Times*, *The Sun*, *The Financial Times* and *the Herald Tribune*.

Television

South Africa has had television only since 1976. The South African Broadcasting Corporation (SABC) provides three television channels: SABC 1 broadcasts in English; SABC 2 and SABC 3 broadcast in eight African languages and in Afrikaans.

Radio

South Africa has numerous radio stations broadcasting in all 11 official languages. As well as SABC's public stations, there are 14 commercial stations and countless community stations.

What's On

The local daily newspapers – *The Argus* in particular – are a good source of listings. The monthly magazine *SA City Life* is a comprehensive guide to what's on not only in Cape Town but other major cities as well.

USEFUL INFORMATION

Tourist Information

Cape Town Tourism
Corner of Castle and Burg Street,
Cape Town 8001
Tel: 021-426 4267/8
www.cape-town.org
Open: daily 8am–7pm.

Capetown Tourism
Shop 107
Clocktower Precinct
Victoria & Alfred Waterfront
Tel: 021-405 4500
www.cape-town.net
Open: daily 9am–6pm

Consulates

Australian Embassy
292 Orient Street
Arcadia
Pretoria
Tel: 0800 993 511

Canadian Consulate
19th Floor, South African Reserve Bank,
60 St George's Mall, Cape Town 8001
Tel: 021-423 5240
www.canada.co.za

British Consulate
15th Floor, Southern Life Building,
8 Riebeek Street, Cape Town 8001
Tel: 021-405 2400
www.britishhighcommission.gov.uk

US Consulate
7th Floor, Broadway Building,
Hertzog Boulevard, Cape Town 8001
Tel: 021-421 4280

Gay and Lesbian

Cape Town is the gay capital of South Africa, and it attracts many like-minded people throughout the year. There are plenty of bars and other venues for gays and lesbians; check out the monthly listings magazine, *SA City Life*. The National Gay and Lesbian Coalition (tel: 011-487 3810/1/2; www.equality.org.za) is the local help and advisory board.

FURTHER READING

Insight Guide: South Africa. Apa Publications. Guidebook combining comprehensive information about all facets of the country with stunning photographs.

Platter, John, *South African Wines 2001*. The Platter Wine Guide SA Pty Ltd. A pocket book that is updated every year. This is an essential local reference book for wine connoisseurs. It covers South African wine estates and their produce, and includes background historical information and glossaries.
Hammond-Tooke, David, *The Roots of Black South Africa*. Jonathan Ball. Fascinating study of southern Africa's cultural traditions; gives the background stories to the artefacts you're likely to be offered in the markets.
Duncan, Paul, *The Illustrated Long Walk to Freedom*. Little, Brown. Revised version of Nelson Mandela's epic, and now legendary work. This Mandela biography also serves as an arresting account of modern South Africa's miserable, sectarian history.
Ramphele, Mamphela, *A Bed Called Home: Life in the Migrant Labour Hostels of Cape Town*. Ohio University Press. The writer, an anthropologist, interviewed a number of the city's hostel dwellers for this profound study of poverty and ways in which the victims can create better lives for themselves.
Nasson, Bill, *Abraham Esau's War: A Black South African War in the Cape, 1899-1902* Cambridge University Press. The Boer War (1899–1902) seen from a black perspective, and focusing on the context of Cape Colony social culture and political life at the turn of the 20th century. A large number of blacks fought in the conflict but were not allowed to share the fruits of peace.

practical information

credits

ACKNOWLEDGEMENTS

Photography	**Bill Wassman** *and*
75	**Hein von Horsten**
16B	**Guy Stubbs**/ABPL
14, 15	**Topham Picture Point**
16T	**Lisa Trocchi**/ABPL
Cover	**Chad Ehlers/Stone/Getty Images**

Cartography	**Berndtson & Berndtson Productions**

© APA Publications GmbH & Co. Verlag KG Singapore Branch, Singapore

Left: Llandudno, Cape Town

INSIGHT
Pocket Guides

Insight Pocket Guides pioneered a new approach to guidebooks, introducing the concept of the authors as "local hosts" who would provide readers with personal recommendations, just as they would give honest advice to a friend who came to stay. They also included a full-size pull-out map. Now, to cope with the needs of the 21st century, new editions in this growing series are being given a new look to make them more practical to use, and restaurant and hotel listings have been greatly expanded.

☀INSIGHT GUIDES

The world's largest collection of visual travel guides

Now in association with

Discovery
CHANNEL®

Also from Insight Guides...

Insight Guides is the classic series, providing the complete picture with expert and informative text and stunning photography. Each book is an ideal travel planner, a reliable on-the-spot companion – and a superb visual souvenir of a trip. 193 titles.

Insight Maps are designed to complement the guidebooks. They provide full mapping of major destinations, and their laminated finish gives them ease of use and durability. 100 titles.

Insight Compact Guides are handy reference books, modestly priced yet comprehensive. The text, pictures and maps are all cross-referenced, making them ideal books to consult while seeing the sights. 127 titles.

INSIGHT POCKET GUIDE TITLES

Aegean Islands
Algarve
Alsace
Amsterdam
Athens
Atlanta
Bahamas
Baja Peninsula
Bali
Bali Bird Walks
Bangkok
Barbados
Barcelona
Bavaria
Beijing
Berlin
Bermuda
Bhutan
Boston
Brisbane & the
    Gold Coast
British Columbia
Brittany
Brussels
Budapest
California,
    Northern

Canton
Cape Town
Chiang Mai
Chicago
Corfu
Corsica
Costa Blanca
Costa Brava
Costa del Sol
Costa Rica
Crete
Croatia
Denmark
Dubai
Fiji Islands
Florence
Florida
Florida Keys
French Riviera
    (Côte d'Azur)
Gran Canaria
Hawaii
Hong Kong
Hungary
Ibiza
Ireland
Ireland's Southwest

Israel
Istanbul
Jakarta
Jamaica
Kathmandu Bikes
    & Hikes
Kenya
Kraków
Kuala Lumpur
Lisbon
Loire Valley
London
Los Angeles
Macau
Madrid
Malacca
Maldives
Mallorca
Malta
Manila
Melbourne
Mexico City
Miami
Montreal
Morocco
Moscow
Munich

Nepal
New Delhi
New Orleans
New York City
New Zealand
Oslo and Bergen
Paris
Penang
Perth
Phuket
Prague
Provence
Puerto Rico
Quebec
Rhodes
Rome
Sabah
St. Petersburg
San Diego
San Francisco
Sarawak
Sardinia
Scotland
Seville, Cordoba &
    Granada
Seychelles
Sicily

Sikkim
Singapore
Southeast England
Southern Spain
Sri Lanka
Stockholm
Switzerland
Sydney
Tenerife
Thailand
Tibet
Toronto
Tunisia
Turkish Coast
Tuscany
Venice
Vienna
Vietnam
Yogjakarta
Yucatán Peninsula

INDEX